DALLAS STOUDENMIRE

The Western Frontier Library

Leon C. Metz

DALLAS STOUDENMIRE

El Paso Marshal

University of Oklahoma Press

Norman

By Leon C. Metz:

John Selman, Texas Gunfighter (New York, 1966)
Pat Garrett: The Story of a Western Lawman (Norman, 1974)
Dallas Stoudenmire: El Paso Marshal (Austin, 1969; Norman, 1979)

Library of Congress Catalog Card Number: 70–79109

To MARLENE,

> *for the neglected years and the*
> *lost opportunities, with*
> *her father's affection*

CONTENTS

		Prologue	xi
CHAPTER	1	Wanted—a Town tamer	1
	2	El Paso in transition	11
	3	Stoudenmire—the early years	24
	4	Four dead men in five seconds	34
	5	Attempted assassination	48
	6	The Railroad comes to Town	55
	7	Crime busting—El Paso style	61
	8	Stoudenmire's feud with the Texas Rangers	70
	9	The strange life & death of	
		Stanley M. "Doc" Cummings	82
	10	The Stoudenmire—Manning Brothers feud	92
	11	Stoudenmire's Political feud	100
	12	Prelude to a gunfight	109
	13	A gunfight at Frank Mannings Saloon	114
	14	End of an era	119
	15	Day of judgement	125
		Footnotes	129
		Bibliography	147
		Acknowledgements	153
		Index	157

ILLUSTRATIONS

Between Pages 60 and 61

Ed Scotten
William Hale
John Hale Family
Dallas Stoudenmire
James B. Gillett and L. S. Turnbo
Capt. George W. Baylor
The Gem Saloon
Dallas Stoudenmire
Stoudenmire's Gun
El Paso Street
W. W. Mills
Joseph Magoffin
"Doc" Manning
James Manning
George Felix "Doc" Manning Family
James Manning Family and Frank Manning
The Lone Star, El Paso's first modern newspaper
Unidentified photograph found on Stoudenmire's body

PROLOGUE

DALLAS STOUDENMIRE was a gunfighter—an auburn-headed, fiery-eyed, six-foot, two-inch container of laughter, liquor, and death. Of all the old-time gunmen, he probably loved living the most. Still, when the occasion arose, he could terminate a man's life as easily as discarding an empty Bull Durham sack. Western history has barely noted Stoudenmire's passing or his accomplishments, but for two tumultuous years in the early 1880's he served as nearly the only law north of the Rio Grande and west of Fort Worth.

Prior to Dallas Stoudenmire's arrival in El Paso, Texas, there existed no authority except that of the six-shooter and very little precedent for a peace officer to follow. Lawlessness and corruption and vice and sin and disorder prevailed. Nevertheless, Stoudenmire accepted the job as city marshal.

He accepted the duty with high hopes and jammed the cornerstone of law and order under the community. Yet history has dismissed him as merely a gunfighter and a drunken one at that. His idealism, enthusiasm, and devotion to duty have been overlooked or ignored. No one remembers what he stood for, only the number of men he killed and how he died.

Dallas Stoudenmire could have been great. Although pitfalls went with the job, so did opportunity. Somehow, though, he failed to take advantage of the position's more positive aspects. Within a year and a half he lay dead with a prostitute's lip rouge on his shirt, a curse on his breath, whiskey on his clothes, and a bullet in his head.

The El Paso that Dallas Stoudenmire sought to tame was created by the railroads, by the wooden cars that carried gamblers, prostitutes, Sunday School teachers, bankers, cattlemen, soldiers, and miners. They stopped at a sleepy little adobe crossroads on an old Spanish trail, a mud village that had been a sun-baked trading post for creaky wagons trekking between Mexico City and Santa Fe. Out of their brawling, working, conniving, and sweating; out of their cheating, drinking, cursing, and dying a town was built—a town in which saloons and whorehouses outnumbered churches a hundred to one.

Stoudenmire made a great many enemies. Strong and fearless men always do. The Texas Rangers disliked him and the politicians feared him. He answered them insult for insult, threat for threat. But towering above his animosity for these two factions loomed his implacable hatred of four men who completely dominated the gambling and prostitution interests in El Paso, the Manning brothers. At least once he and the Mannings patched up their quarrel, but the fissure ran too deep. Only death would end the conflict.

Dallas Stoudenmire bears much of the blame for these troubles. He was a prideful man, and an overabundance of this pride toppled him from the city marshal's position. Pride led him to seek revenge as one killing led to counter killings. In the end, pride killed him.

His driving motives were of the purest, even if his methods were not the best. Few doubted his dedication and devotion to duty. If trying to bring peace to an ungrateful town while constantly facing the spectre of assassination made an alcoholic and an unconscionable killer out of him, it would probably have done the same to any man in his situation.

chapter 1 WANTED—A TOWN TAMER

D ALLAS STOUDENMIRE was not El Paso's first marshal, but he offered his credentials at an opportune time. No qualified individuals were available and the city fathers were agreeing more and more that the path to growth would have to be paved with the bodies of its toughest citizens. That decision reached, the remaining problem was to hire a gunman with no conscience in his trigger finger.

El Paso's law enforcement had jumped off to a dismal start. Saloon gossip at Paul Keating's Saloon and John Doyle's establishment had it that the town could not acquire a gunfighter powerful enough to curry its wicked ways. When the present crop of city marshals had been tested and discarded, the rough element intended to push George Campbell. Bill Johnson, the town drunkard, was also mentioned.

The village troubles had originated back in 1873 when El Paso received its charter of incorporation from the State of Texas. On August 12, a mayor and city council were installed. In September of 1876, government machinery broke down and the aldermen dismissed themselves. A chronic lack of attendance at council meetings brought about this disgraceful situation.

On July 3, 1880, a new shoe was nailed onto the political foot of El Paso. Solomon Schutz became mayor. Aldermen were Joseph Magoffin, B. S. Dowell, A. Kraukauer, T. D. Ochoa, Antonio Hart, and S. C. Slade. Although problems were monumental, the most pressing was law enforcement. On July 26, 1880, John B. Tays was appointed by the city council to be El Paso's first marshal.

Tays had recently established a dubious sort of fame. He became the only Texas Ranger commander in history to surrender his forces, the event becoming part of a clash of weapons known as the El Paso Salt War.[1]

On August 3 the aldermen voted Tays an assistant named John Woods, a blacksmith.[2] Neither Tays nor Woods drew a salary because of the city's hampered financial condition. Both had to live on earnings from their normal occupations, plus their share of fees for arrests. By their very nature these duties made few friends for the officers.

Tays had other chores in addition to being marshal. He had to keep the streets clean and fit for travel.

North of El Paso towered the Franklin Mountains, the lower portion thrusting its boulder-strewn rim into the outskirts of the city. Rain runoff was always a critical problem. During a heavy downpour, torrents of water would rage down the *arroyos*, inundating nearly everything. Each time the water sloshed through, a few weak adobe structures disappeared with it. Fortunately, these buildings were, for the most part, constructed out of the soil on which they stood, so the land had barely baked dry before they were all standing again.

Street repairs became a pressing problem. After a deluge, ragged potholes appeared in the caliche and sand roads; the junction of El Paso and San Antonio Streets became a quagmire. When the earth dried, the marshal took the responsibility for rebuilding the thoroughfares. Jail labor was used. Those prisoners who had not contributed financially to the officers' support by payment of their fines were sentenced to pick and shovel their way out of confinement by filling the holes with rocks and dirt.

Another method of road building (and one not too popular with the citizenry) was to fill the space with refuse. This practice led to the dismissal of Tays and Woods.

Trouble developed when John Tays had a large amount of trash dumped in a hole at the foot of San Francisco Street. The council seemed little impressed by this unimaginative highway engineering and on August 17 instructed Woods that the mess had to be cleaned up at Tays' own expense.[3]

Council minutes do not indicate the effectiveness of this order, but they do show that on October 25 both Tays and Woods were removed from their positions.

A. I. Stevens, a forty-seven-year-old wagon and carriage maker,[4] was next appointed marshal. His assistant was drunken Bill Johnson.

Stevens apparently had his faults also. In addition to his duties as town marshal, his chores included the functions of city tax assessor and collector. On November 26, the city fathers removed him for "neglect and dereliction of duty."[5] They published no details.

Now the community had picked its way through most of the contenders and had sifted its way down to a gentleman supported heavily by the saloon crowds. George Campbell, a remarkable young Kentuckian, sought and obtained the marshal's badge. A man with a fair education and from a respectable family, Campbell (according to some El Pasoans) under happier circumstances might have become a valuable citizen.[6] After leaving Kentucky following the Civil War, he journeyed to Young County, Texas, and served a short stint as deputy sheriff.[7] Then he came directly to El Paso.

It was on the recommendation of Captain George Baylor, commander of the company of Texas Rangers stationed at Ysleta, that Campbell was appointed marshal.[8] There is thus some reason to suspect that Campbell had earlier served in the Texas Rangers and had attracted the Captain's admiration. However, the official files (incomplete) of the Texas Rangers do not mention his name. At any rate, on December 1, 1880, George Campbell became El Paso's third marshal. Bill Johnson was still the acting assistant.

Marshal Campbell has had his champions, few as they have been. Mr. W. M. Coldwell, respected pioneer El Pasoan who knew George Campbell, commented in a newspaper review of James Gillett's *Six Years with the Texas Rangers* that "Campbell [was] by no means vicious or naturally lawless [although he] was closely connected with men of the element he was supposed to control. He was ... too unsophisticated and too upright to levy blackmail, and his connection with the disturbers of the public order was too intimate to make it a pleasant duty for him to be energetic in their arrest, conviction, and suppression."

Certainly Campbell appeared to be a different breed of man from any of the previous marshals. The sporting element admired him and he was probably more quick and deadly with a gun than any of his predecessors. In addition, his former role as a deputy sheriff indicates that he may have had some experience at man killing.

Nevertheless, this utterance by Coldwell that the marshal was "too upright to levy blackmail" is noteworthy considering the action that Campbell took in trying to draw a salary.

Campbell's official position put him in a financial quandary. What money he pocketed came from arrest fees, and most of the law-breakers were his friends. Understandably, they did not appreciate the situation and neither did he.

As a result of the marshal's hesitation, the rattletrap jail (simply a room in a vacant house), usually stayed cluttered with tramps, drifters, and others residing near the bottom rungs of the social and financial ladders. Their fines, when they could afford to pay anything at all, did nothing toward providing Campbell and Johnson with improved standards of living.

So the city of El Paso found itself with a reluctant marshal. Law enforcement lagged noticeably. There occurred no stampede of applicants to seize Campbell's job, so the marshal sat quietly in his office and waited for the council to use good judgment and pay him.

The council refused to part with any money until they had exhausted every excuse in their political book. First there would be an attempt to bring in the Texas Rangers and have them patrol the town. The sole expense would be hay for the ranger horses. With Marshal Campbell sitting in attendance, the aldermen sent the following message to Governor Roberts on December 23, 1880:[9]

Sir:

We the Mayor and Board of Aldermen of the City of El Paso, having under consideration the ways and means . . . to better administer the law and city ordinance, to preserve order, and to protect life and property within the city limits . . . [note] that the time has now come when . . . [we] are unable to protect life and property. And the reasons for such inability we respectfully assign the following:

1st. That the sheriff of this county and his deputies . . . reside fifteen miles distant.

2nd. A Marshal and Assistant Marshal, together with one Constable, constitute the police force of this city. The force is not stronger for the want of funds . . . to provide compensation for police officers, and to maintain the municipal government.

3rd. The Southern Pacific and the Rio Grande and El Paso Railways are on the eve of completion to this point. As the forerunners and followers of such enterprises, we now have turned loose upon us hordes of vagabonds, gamblers, burglars, thieves, and particularly murderers.

4th. Like classes have also poured into El Paso, Mexico, one mile distant . . . and thus one place is a refuge for criminals and fugitives of the other. We have no doubt that in each of the El Pasos, confederates for crime are now being formed, with aids and confederates in the other.

Therefore, to the end that law may be enforced, peace and good order be preserved, and life and property be protected, we respectfully request that Colonel G. W. Baylor and his detachment of State forces now stationed at Ysleta, be ordered here for the purpose of aiding the municipal authority until such time as the municipality shall be able . . . to execute the law and its ordinances.

The governor's answer to this plea for assistance has not been preserved, but on January 6, 1881, Major John B. Jones ordered Captain Baylor to "make arrangements for quarters [at El Paso] and move your company to that place."[10] Jones noted that the State "could not pay for the extravagant rents charged for houses in El Paso, there being no appropriation for such purposes [but] . . . the

Mayor and aldermen of El Paso propose to furnish quarters for yourself and men if you will call upon them before moving."

Living quarters in El Paso proved to be as scarce as honest citizens. Finally a deal was worked out where the rangers would occupy free of charge the Marsh Ranch, four and one half miles below El Paso.[11] Several rangers were assigned daily to assist Campbell and Johnson in enforcing the peace.

In the meantime, Captain Baylor wrote his commanding officer that the council had agreed to pay Campbell a salary, the size of which Baylor did not divulge.[12] If this was so, the aldermen were keeping the promise a secret because the minutes make no mention of the alleged transaction. Nevertheless, Campbell patiently waited for the money and when it did not arrive, he filed suit against the city and won his case (this also according to Baylor). However, in spite of legal action, he never drew a cent.

The council could have paid something. It is true that taxes were uncollectable until the city corporation had passed its first year, but the town had other methods of raising revenue and took full advantage of them. A system of fees helped clear the monetary hurdle: fortune tellers paid $100; traveling physicians, surgeons, and occultists paid $25 to practice their trade. A dramatic presentation was charged $5.50, a circus $25, and fights between men and bulls, dogs and bulls, and bears and dogs cost $250 for each performance.[13] In addition to this, one of the largest sources of municipal income was the prostitutes—their fees were $10 each per month.

The list goes on and on, and as is usual with fees, the rates for all such practices tended to rise. So the city government, if not rich, was at least not in poverty.

Knowing that the city was not broke created some bitter feelings inside Marshal Campbell. In anger over the shoddy treatment, he devised a scheme which would rock the town all the way from the Rio Grande to the soon-to-be-completed Southern Pacific railroad tracks. A tight-fisted municipality was going to acknowledge that law and order would cost money.

The plan proved deceptively simple. The El Paso "hard faction" would tree the city. Windows would be shattered, signs would be ripped down, and terror would predominate. Then as the crash of gunfire rose in intensity, the town would be forced to negotiate with Campbell to halt the disorders. The price for compliance would be a regular monthly salary.

Campbell had the full support of the town toughs. These men had everything to gain and only a night's sleep to lose; they would burn the community down if necessary to keep him in office. Their reasons, of course, were logical. If Campbell stayed, the gunmen would be assured of favorable treatment; if Campbell left, someone less understanding of their position might insist that they obey the laws.

On approximately the first of January, 1881, at about two o'clock one morning, the El Paso residents were jolted out of their sleep by city wide convulsions of gunfire. A mob roared back and forth through the streets. The door of Alderman Kraukauer's *domicilio* was knocked sagging with numerous bullet impacts. The home of Mayor Schutz was treated nearly as unkindly. Joseph Magoffin tucked his long, white beard close to his chest and bottled up his home as securely as possible.

It is not precisely known if Campbell took an active part in the riot. At least he did nothing to stop it.

The whereabouts of Assistant Marshal Johnson during the uproar is unknown. He may have left town or he may have assisted with the pistol shooting. A more realistic judgment of his behavior would be that he lay drunk somewhere, completely oblivious and unconcerned about all that was taking place. It is interesting to note that the council never held him responsible for the riot.

Understandably, the mayor and aldermen were nearly prostrate with fear. Meeting furtively, they dispatched a rider to the rangers. Immediate assistance was requested.

Captain Baylor read the plea and instructed Sergeant Gillett to take Corporal Lloyd and a detail of four men,[14] collect fifteen days' rations, and report for duty to the mayor of El Paso. Charging George Campbell with assault with intent to murder, a warrant was placed in Gillett's hands. However, word of the ranger movements raced ahead and the marshal fled to the safety of Johnny Hale's ranch, which lay along the Rio Grande a few miles northwest of El Paso and near the New Mexico territorial line.

Gillett remained in El Paso only long enough to

establish civil law, then returned to camp. Left in charge of the town were Rangers Weldon and Johnson (no known relation to the assistant marshal), who Baylor later admitted were friendly with the hard faction.

When Campbell learned that Sergeant Gillett had left, he returned to El Paso in a hack and drunkenly rode up and down El Paso Street, firing his pistol in the air. In loud and abusive terms he threatened to take the life of Mayor Schutz. Rangers Weldon and Johnson were amused by his antics. Johnson grinned and handed Campbell the warrant signed by Judge Magoffin, but the ranger made no effort to place the marshal in chains.

George Campbell seemed amused also. He hacked and spit, seized the warrant and read it loudly. Then he paused mementarily to scribble some obscenities on it. Turning the horses around, he lashed them down El Paso Street, all the while screaming and threatening to kill Magoffin.

Of course the judge had no intention of even allowing his beard to poke through the portals of his residence. As soon as Campbell realized that his challenges were going unheeded and unanswered, he turned and rode back to Hale's ranch.

Everyone laughed; the last few days had been hilarious. Captain Baylor proved to be the only sour note. When he learned what had happened, he spurred his horse into El Paso and called T. L. Weldon and William Johnson to account.

"Campbell is a personal friend . . . [and we] thought that he was in the right . . . [and] did not wish to arrest him," Johnson muttered.

"This will not do for rangers," Baylor snorted. "You should arrest a brother if a warrant is placed in your hands for him."[15]

Baylor handed both rangers their discharges. Johnson reportedly left the country. T. L. Weldon bitterly rode to Hale's ranch where he joined forces with Marshal Campbell and Chris Peveler, another ranger who had previously incurred Baylor's wrath and had been thrown out of the company.

By January 14, charges were dropped against Marshal Campbell and he was allowed to resign. At the same council meeting Ed Copeland, owner and proprietor of the Occidental Saloon, was sworn in to fill the vacant marshal's post. For the first time, compensation in the amount of fifty dollars a month was attached to the job.

William Johnson, hanging on to his liquor bottle, once again received the nod to be the assistant marshal. Bill's father was "Old Man Johnson," universally esteemed throughout the city. It was because of the old man that the son became a deputy. Bill's salary was fixed at forty dollars a month and each lawman was still entitled to collect fees for arrests.

With compensation attached to the position of marshal, the city officials felt they could be a little stricter about whom they employed. The new marshal was required to post a five hundred dollar bond. Right away this ruling made a casualty out of Marshal Copeland. He had barely polished his badge before he lost it. Appparently he could not furnish bond. At the February 14 city council meeting, it was agreed among the aldermen that Copeland had not fully qualified and he was dismissed.

With the office of marshal now vacant, Bill Johnson seemed the only person left to appoint. Chomping on their mustaches in frustration, the council gave him the job. What else could they do until a qualified man came along? Right now he was the sole individual in town who even wanted the job.

Johnson's presence in El Paso meant absolutely nothing where the lawless factions were concerned. Daily shootings were the rule rather than the exception. Honest citizens were harrassed and forced to endure the indignities common to all cities held in the grasp of mob rule. The rangers, of course, kept the jails full, even though they could not quell the disturbances completely. On February 11, Corporal Harrison and four rangers caught some bad-men by surprise and made nineteen arrests.[16] On March 1, Corporal Lloyd and four men made two arrests,[17] and on the fifteenth Privates Beaumont, Wilson, and Danipien netted over a dozen.[18]

Baylor was unable to spare enough men to completely clean up the town or even keep it quiet. Most of his rangers were kept busy tracking and fighting Indians, and six men were generally the limit that could be sent to El Paso. Oftentimes, on nights that were particularly violent and noisy, Baylor himself would hasten to El Paso in order to put down the latest outbreaks. He noted on April 5:

"I have quite a time watching El Paso. I went up [last] night . . . [with a] doublebarreled shotgun and had two men armed the same way. We tried to catch the rowdies shooting in the streets, but they smelled a rat and kept quiet. They came near shooting Judge Blacker's thirteen year old daughter through the head. I wanted to everlastingly shoot the daylights out of them."[19]

Obviously the rangers were a help, but not an answer to El Paso's crime wave. So the city fathers began actively searching for a town-tamer; and for the first time they started scouring the countryside for a gunman. This caused a ripple of consternation across the El Paso *Times* which was familiar with this method of law enforcement in other Western towns. On April 2, 1881, the *Times* remarked in an editorial: "Who will guard the guardians? is the prime consideration in selecting a suitable marshal to police the city. We want him sober and discreet as well as fearless."

The same issue also carried the notation that two petitions were being heavily signed and made ready for the city council. Being recommended for the position of marshal were a Mr. True and a Mr. Dallas Stoudenmire.

On April 11, the resignation of Marshal William Johnson was read and approved in the council chambers. Mr. True's nomination received no consideration. Dallas Stoudenmire was chosen with one dissenting vote. His salary was set at one hundred dollars a month with no fees,[20] although this ruling was later changed and he was paid fees also.

chapter 2   EL PASO IN TRANSITION

E L PASO MARSHAL Dallas Stoudenmire in-
herited three dilemmas in relation to the problems of law enforcement.
A portion of the Texas, New Mexico, and Old Mexico boundaries
shoved themselves into a tight little cross section near one point, El
Paso. Here two different cultures and three different political systems
wrestled to blend together (New Mexico was still a territory). Outlaws
whose normal habitat lay on one side or the other of these hazily drawn
lines had only to step across and be safe on the other. Number two was
the remoteness of El Paso, the isolation exerting an evil influence on
those disposed to breaking the law. And last loomed the lack of any
final arbitrator except the six-shooter.

        Although Stoudenmire's long legs could in ten min-
utes stride over every mesquite bush inside his official arena of
authority, what he saw was only now emerging from centuries of
crumbling tradition. This vast region still felt the influence of Spanish
custom. Decades before, the soft sand had crunched beneath the supple
leather sandals of the humble padres bringing salvation to the Jumano,
Piro, Tompiro, and Tigua Indians. They also, with varying degrees of

success, attempted to establish the Cross of God among the more hostile Apaches and Comanches.

El Paso could have become one of the oldest settlements in the United States if in 1598 *Don Juan De Onate* had paused on the north bank of the Rio Grande (then called the *Rio Bravo* and various other titles) and claimed the area for Spain. Instead he halted on the south bank thirty miles or so below what is now Juarez, Mexico, and sweepingly proclaimed ownership of all the terrain for His Catholic Majesty Phillip II.[1] Onate called this particular region Paso del Norte, signifying the north passage through the mountains. By the late 1650's, a small village had sprung up.

Nothing along the border is more ancient than Paso del Norte unless it is the alternately savage and gentle Rio Grande, the pounding silence of the vastness, the cutting sharpness of the dust-laden wind, or the ragged grandeur of the barren mountain ranges. Here were the trading posts, the large adobe houses of the well-to-do, and the hovels of the poor. By any building standards, the village did not qualify as an oasis of beauty. Although many prosperous residents whitewashed their homes, the huts (and huts were the predominant buildings) were generally of one monotonous color—muddy brown. The insides of the houses appeared exactly similar to the outsides, except that they were a little harder to see after leaving the relentless glare of the sun. Plaster blessed no walls and anything but a dirt floor was unheard of. The homes and buildings did have one life-giving ingredient, however; due to the thickness and insulation of the mud walls, the dwellings were refreshingly comfortable in the summer and easy to heat in the winter.

Along the main thoroughfare, *Calle Comercio* (Commerce Street—later to be called *Calle 16th de Septiembre* in honor of the Mexican 4th of July), the row of buildings supported and clung to each other, giving the impression of massive fortress walls extending for blocks. Only gun ports were missing to make the effect complete. During the heat of the afternoon it was easy to assume that the villagers were dead or that Paso del Norte was deserted. That wasn't so. The inhabitants had retired to the interior of their huts and were resting until the simmering sun disappeared behind the mountains.

One remarkedly attractive structure stood out like a

blooming desert flower among the greasewood. That is, it looked attractive if consideration was taken that for five hundred miles in any lonesome direction there was nothing of man-made loveliness to compare with it. The *Mission de Nuestra Senora de Guadalupe* claimed a bell tower, making the church unique among the flat roofed structures. Completely dominating the religious and non-religious life of the Mexican peasants (and to a certain extent of the Americans as well), the mission became the one area of stabilizing influence. If during the past week a man had been sent to Hell via the bullet-strewn path, everyone attended Mass on Sunday and solemnly prayed for his unfortunate soul.

The Mexican community ran full of gun-toting, hard-drinking sinners. In spite of the overshadowing presence of the mission, the saloons and *cantinas* furnished the community's excitement. One establishment that had more dread than appeal, however, was the *carcel*. The jail was geared for Mexican political prisoners, but neither the police nor garrison soldier guards seemed reluctant about incarcerating others. In particular, the latch string was always out for the *Gringo pistoleros* from the bordering community of El Paso.

El Paso (sometimes incorrectly called Franklin or Magoffsinville) lay about one mile north of the Rio Grande and appeared in many respects to be merely an adobe copy of its older sister across the river. In 1827 *Juan Maria Ponce de Leon* petitioned the Mexican authorities for a plot of land in what is now the center of El Paso; then it was simply a worthless area known for its mud flats. In 1846 Colonel Doniphan and his farm boys smashed a Mexican force near El Paso and the northern region beyond the Rio Grande slipped forever from the feeble grasp of Mexico.

In 1849 El Paso became a waystation for forty-niners hurrying to the gold fields of California. Then after a brief burst of activity during the Civil War, the village slept until 1880, only rarely being jarred out of its slumber by gunfire, the most notable exchange coming during the Salt War.

Prior to 1880, El Paso had a population of less than five hundred souls, lost and otherwise, all of whom lived in what the Las Vegas (New Mexico) *Optic* of February 28, 1881, called the "jumping off place of creation," a country "equal to the orthodox church belief in Hell." The newspaper thought El Paso enchanting when viewed from a distance of fifty to sixty miles, but "any view closer than that reveals nothing but sand hills, the most barren waste imaginable with but a few mud houses, and a scant supply of cottonwoods trying to relieve the oppressive monotony."

But the *Optic* agreed that change was bustling about in the dust laden winds. The town was still the "worst hole" in the Southwest, but it was a profitable one. Las Vegas reporters noted that St. Louis capitalists were nosing around the border community and purchasing land, driving the prices skyward. Already, town lots were selling for between $1500 and $2500 apiece. The boom was on to such an extent that a shortage of building materials existed. And by the end of 1881, money and people had so completely altered the town that the El Paso *Times* reported a bustling population of "American, 1600; Mexican, 600; Chinese, 300; and colored, 100."[2]

Of course, not all of these folks were desirable citizens. "Imagine the main street of San Angelo," Judge Pruess said upon returning to that city, "with all the houses flat roofed, and about a thousand drunken men, railroad hands, gamblers, and adventurers, all swaggering, fighting, and yelling through the streets and you have a pretty good idea of El Paso as it is."[3]

Judge Pruess was an observant and truthful man. Many of the newcomers were destined to barely get settled before being transferred to Concordia Cemetery. Unlike the one or two small graveyards along the northern extremes of El Paso, Concordia lay near the eastern section and could expand forty miles to the Hueco Mountains. These potential cemetery customers were lured to the border by the prospects of easy money, lack of law and order, a place to hide, or simply a new way of life. Behind them they left wives, mothers, husbands, sweethearts, friends, fathers, and all too often the sheriff. The magnet of El Paso's isolation tugged at the heart of every disreputable character in the Southwest.

This same isolation also helped the growth of a budding El Paso industry—organized prostitution.

The local union scale ran from fifty cents up to whatever could be badgered—or cajoled—out of man. All of this depended upon a great many factors: the reputation and atmosphere of a bagnio, the status and beauty of the girl, the uniqueness of the wares offered, and how drunk or gullible the man was who had come to see the elephant.

Originally the trade started with Mexican strumpets, but the railroad changed all that. Iron rails brought a variety of goods into El Paso; German, French, British, Hungarian, Chinese, Scandinavian, and Slav girls poured into town, seeking a dollar here and a dollar there and, incidentally, supporting the city treasury. The more ingenious nymphs of the tenderloin district regularly thought up new methods of advertising business, not unlike the supermarkets of today. There were doorway demonstrations, more was offered for the money, rates slid up and down according to the supply and demand schedules of paydays, and additional services were a passable substitute for double-stamp day. On March 17 a young lady in one house of mirth dyed her hair green in honor of Saint Patrick.

The cribs along the streets were a constant source of embarrassment to the police department. Officers and Texas Rangers, along with city politicians and merchants, made it a regular part of their daily schedule to dally somewhere along the line for liquid and female refreshments. And yet the law still had to be enforced. Brawls and drunkenness were always a part of the scene.

On August 9, 1882, a very drunk fellow by the name of Brothers entered the lodgings of one Hannah Burns and soon fell asleep in the comfort of Hannah's charms. While lying there, sublime and smiling, he had $175 in gold disappear. Early the next morning, a very irate Mr. Brothers stormed into the police station and angrily told Gillett that "Hannah had taken unwarranted liberties with his pockets." Gillett assigned Assistant Marshal Comstock to the case.

The *Lone Star* snickered at Comstock's actions, claiming "His pleasant relations with the accused gave assurance that the search proceedings would be conducted with that delicacy due to the refinement and culture of the suspected Hannah." Naturally, no money was found.

Comstock did have his troubles at other times, however. In 1884, he became the bona fide El Paso City Marshal and one evening sallied forth to arrest Adela Guzman, a Mexican siren working at Gipsie Davenport's. Adela resented Comstock's attentions (which we assume were perfectly legal) and fired a shot at the marshal. Comstock stepped aside as the bullet slammed into a wall; then he tossed Miss Guzman in jail and set her bond at $350. That night she broke out and escaped to Mexico, the *Lone Star* noting that she was now "basking in the sunlight of the land of God and Liberty."

Of course, the harlots were not the only ladies causing trouble; respectable wives often did their share. One prominent businessman, whom the *Lone Star* declined to name, on January 24, 1883, rushed into a saloon while brandishing a pistol. His condition appeared very excited and nervous, as well it might. "He had just discovered his wife in very close proximity with a neighbor inside a privy." There exist no details concerning the fate of the wife and neighbor, but the cuckolded husband's excitement appeared possibly dangerous, and officers arrested him for carrying a gun.

Respectable women were often taken for harlots. Once, a stranger insulted a very proper young lady as she sat in the window of her home trying to catch a whiff of the cool evening air. Her son, standing unnoticed just inside the premises, became enraged, grabbed a revolver, rushed outside and crashed the gun barrel down between the ruffian's ears. "Glad to hear about this firm action," the *Lone Star* dryly commented.

But the prostitutes did constitute a nuisance and sometimes even had the gall to believe they were as good as the righteous folks. It was considered atrocious manners if one appeared on the streets. Simeon Newman, the eloquent hell-raising editor of the *Lone Star*, constantly railed at the girls for their vulgarity. "A few days ago we saw a carriage loaded down with three or four of them, plus men, all drunk, and shouting vile language. It stopped in front of the post office and the women used filthy language to parties they talked to on the street. A day or so later we saw another on the platform of a street car smoking a cigar and talking with the driver in such language. The law ought to be rigidly enforced against these people until they are cured of flaunting their sin in the respectable portion of the community."

For thunder against the more repulsive types of depravity, it was simply hard to beat the virtuous pen of Simeon Newman. His *Lone Star* fought vice so continuously and relentlessly that the criminal element finally warned the merchants to either quit advertising in the *Lone Star* or face a boycott. The threat proved successful, and the *Lone Star* folded, saying, "Every gambler, pimp, and whore will celebrate our closing."

Fights in the brothels became such a common occurrence that people were becoming concerned. One example is that of Ann Myers, the madam at 444 Utah Street (now Mesa Avenue). Ann brawled with Lou Howard, tore Lou's dress, wrenched her arm, pistol whipped her, and threatened murder.

The citizens were objecting also to the practice of scarlet ladies riding through the streets at all hours. Noise finally became so disagreeable that during March, July, and August of 1885 the city council was presented with a petition asking that the prostitutes be restricted to a certain section of the city. The whores were now regulated and on the run. Although their finest hour had not yet arrived, in retrospect this action by the city council marked the beginning of their exile from El Paso.

Fines (or rather dues) were prescribed in the sum of $10 each per month. Of course, the prostitutes organized and attempted to fight back. Etta Clark, Verdie Love, Jane Brown, and several other fallen ladies resisted the payment of monies and petitioned the council for a reduction in fees to $5 per month. Answering, the council referred the matter to the marshal and ordered him to ascertain how many of the signers had paid their fines. All opposition stopped.

From that day forward, the bordellos in El Paso began to take on an air of ornateness. Some of the better-looking and more businesslike whores decided to expand their activities—they avoided the harlot tag and tried to call themselves actresses. Naturally, several theatres immediately sprang up, one of the earliest being the Coliseum Saloon and Variety Theatre. The Gem was another, and one night as several girls danced on stage a group of playful cowboys showered money across the floor and effectively interrupted the performance. On the following night, the cowmen returned, took seats near the stage and being experts with the lariat, pitched out a lasso every time a leg kicked out toward the audience. When a shapely ankle was snarled, the damsel was hauled screaming across the stage—usually refusing to return until law officers had removed the rope artists from their front-row positions.

Near the 1890s, true bordello elegance appeared in El Paso. Tillie Howard opened a world-famous establishment, closely followed in luxury by Pearl Beebe, Cleo Starr, Etta Clark, and May Palmer. Prostitution flourished in circumstances resembling oriental luxury. Even the rugs were softer then the beds of a few years ago. The girls slunk about in expensive silks, satins, and furs—everything for the exquisite entertainment of those who preferred stylish sex and carried more than $5 in their pockets. The correct name of these places was Parlor Houses, although in reality they were men's clubs. Originally they accommodated from twenty to thirty women. All night long, standing in the streets, one could hear the madam welcoming visitors and crying, "Company in the parlor, girls."

Nearly every night brought its wild barrage of gunfire. The *Lone Star* commented that "the people of El Paso are probably the best armed men on the continent today. Principally Winchester rifles and Colt .45s [are carried]." Next to the sellers of ammunition, the undertakers were probably El Paso's busiest merchants.

A good example of this senseless slaughter came about when Attorney Neill borrowed a revolver from saloon owner George Look. Look forgot to mention that the gun had a hair trigger, and Neill neglected to store it in a safe place. As a result, the maid picked up the weapon and began to toy with it. The pistol cracked and Neill's two-year-old child died.

El Paso had no shortage of deliberate deaths to match the accidental ones. Many of these did not even get honorable mention in the newspapers since there was nothing new or unusual in gunfights. In order for an editor to mention a new killing, it either had to have novelty attached or involve someone important. An unusual killing occurred on April 2, 1881.

On this day the El Paso *Times* praised merchant Ben Schuster in the lavish terms that only an old-time newspaper editor could handle. The story was that Eugene O'Connell had been slain a few nights before in a gunfight, the details of which nobody ever bothered to write down. After the corpse had festered a day or two under the copper sun, talk began going around that it should be buried.

Ben Schuster stepped forward. Just because a man died like a dog was no reason for him to be buried like one. He purchased a coffin, an act which earned him the praise of the newspaper.

A coffin in El Paso was as rare as a glacier in the Franklin Mountains. The poor and underprivileged never expected anything more than to be wrapped in a blanket before being tucked gently into the earth. An American girl tagged "Slim Jim" became well known from hanging around the saloons. Suddenly she died. The boys wanted to send her away in style but there was not a casket to be found in all El Paso. George Look finally solved the problem. He had recently received a shipment of wooden doors for his saloon, and with a few nails in the right places, the portals were converted into a makeshift coffin.

Death was truly a tyrant on both sides of the Rio Grande. By any unit of measurement, the gunmen in El Paso and Paso del Norte had filled Hell several times over. Most of these gunfights have long since been forgotten—having been tucked away in faded letters and newspaper files. One of the most deadly, but least known, battles in Western history occurred in El Paso on February 18, 1881. This shoot-out established the precedent which engulfed Dallas Stoudenmire, although he had nothing to do with it. Through no fault of his own, the course of events snatched him up, pushed him toward his greatest fame, and set the stage for his death.

Events began on January 28. A peddler was noticed flashing a large roll of bills in a Paso del Norte cabaret. Some observant Americans took cognizance of this and, not wanting him to fall in with dishonest company, decided to assume charge of his welfare. Everyone went for a stroll and moments later one of the *Americanos* had his hand inside the victim's pocket and was helping himself to what he found there.

"Let's go get a drink," one of the thieves said.

Inside the saloon, the men poured themselves *cervesa* and *tequila*. The guitar pickers were handsomely paid as this beer and liquor flowed. Presently the same wealthy customer passed by again and started displaying large amounts of cash. Exchanging a surprised look, the Americans took their friend by the arm and all went for another walk. This time a hand dug deep into another pocket and an equally large bundle of *pesos* stuck to the finger tips.

That the peddler managed to retain money is the first strange knot in the rope of events that followed. Once again the same thing happened. The intoxicated Mexican staggered into a saloon and happily splashed cash around once more, an act which made the villains feel foolish and did in fact seriously damage their professional reputation among El Paso robbers. Grabbing the fellow under the arms, they carried and dragged him to the lonely desert and stripped his clothes completely off. The pockets and seams underwent a thorough searching and this time the Mexican was out of money. In all, over eight hundred dollars in *pesos* had now changed hands.

By the time the naked fellow had walked back to town, the cool night air had made a sober man out of him. Hurrying straight to the police, he blurted out his nearly unbelievable tale. That night the news flashed out that every American in the city was to be incarcerated. Most of the guilty parties were rounded up; but the dragnet also dropped over several who were innocent.

According to Charles C. Richardson, the American consular official in Paso del Norte, the names of those taken into custody were Frank Thompson, Frank O'Neal, J. C. Cain, Les Davis, Patrick Ryan, Frank Allen, and Hugh Cox.[4]

Saloon owner George Look wrote the names he could remember (after a lapse of twenty-five years) as Nibsy, Thompson, Lafayette Kid, Ryan, and Joe King. Look described these men as belonging to the "gang or hard faction" in El Paso. All of these gunmen were familiar with the inside of a jail—although not accustomed to remaining long. They constituted a rough, undisciplined brigade, fast with their guns as well as with their wits.

This "hard faction" had friends all over El Paso, the most prominent being the Manning brothers. So far only James, Frank, and John were in town. George Felix "Doc" Manning still lived in Belton, Texas, although rapidly making plans to move to El Paso.

Due particularly to the Manning efforts, all of El Paso frothed in ferment over the arrests. Threats were delivered to the Mexican officials, demands which thundered for the immediate release of the prisoners. Consequently, Mexico agreed to hold quick trials so that the innocent could return to their homes.

By February 18, the court cases still had not appeared on the docket and a whisper circulated along El Paso Street that a jail break was imminent. Look first learned of these plans when he strolled into the Lone Star Saloon and the proprietor John Doyle asked if he had an extra forty-five.

"No, I don't," George replied.

"There is one behind the bar that you can have for ten dollars Mexican money. Get it and lay it on the table in the back room—then say nothing. I'll tell you later what's up."[5]

George did as he was told and as he laid down the gun, he noticed that two or three other weapons lay there also. Watching these weapons were several Mexican girls who stood around smoking and talking. Look checked back later and saw that the revolvers were missing. So were the girls.

Mexican custom allowed wives and sweethearts to visit their loved ones who were confined in jail. Special rooms were often set aside for this. On that 18th day of February, several American prisoners received female visitors. Smiling, the guards waved the girls through, not noticing that several seemed more "busty" than usual. Inside each blouse bounced a deadly forty-five.

An adobe fortress, the jail walls were higher than a man's head and circled the entire block. The front entrance, and only exit, was guarded by a squad of soldiers.

Thompson made the first move. He kicked open the gate and started shooting. Down went the captain and one soldier, twisting and squirming in agony along the ground. Another guard rose hastily from where he squatted and was clubbed unconscious.

All the while, Frank Thompson's voice rang out, bellowing demands for the others to follow him. But they were in a quandary, too frightened to run and too frightened to stay. Pat Ryan came cautiously through the door, obviously having second thoughts about leaving. Running as far as a saloon down the street, there his nerve completely failed him. He took cover behind the bar and waited to surrender.

Another, known only as the Lafayette Kid, came charging out, then flipped over an obstruction and rolled into a ditch. Placing his hands over his head, he chose to remain there rather than continue with his escape try.

Only Frank O'Neal and J. C. Cain leaped through the jail entrance and joined Thompson in an honest flight for freedom. Judging by their unhappy fate, they should have remained in prison or surrendered with the others.

As the three men raced across the sandy area north of the prison, they were pursued and overtaken by a *vaquero* who had been eating in a restaurant on the east side of the *plaza de la carcel*. Startled by the shooting, he mounted his horse, removed a rifle from its scabbard, and rode after the escapees. He thus became the only man to stand between the prisoners and liberty, and he overtook them as they were crossing an *acequia* (irrigation ditch).

Thompson, O'Neal, and Cain never had much of a chance. They opened fire at the relentless pursuer but, struggling and falling in chest high water, their aim was wild. The rifle began to crack and all three sank in death beneath the muddy surface.

Later the bodies were recovered and tied to the tails of burros for a victory parade through the center of Paso del Norte. From a high vantage point in El Paso, a viewer could see the three men bounced through the streets. Belt buckles and spurs glinted in the sun as the carrion jolted along across the sharp rocks and chuckholes. The lifeless arms flapped and the mouths hung agape—as if surprised and startled at the sudden death which had so brutally overtaken them.

What was left of the hard faction in El Paso became infuriated over the way the three men had been killed. Vengeance was vowed by many, in particular by James, Frank, and John Manning. The brothers owned a small ranch adjoining Johnny Hale's place (about ten miles above El Paso), and they instructed Hale, who was also their ranch foreman, to be on the lookout for the Mexican responsible for the killing. Oftentimes a Mexican cowboy wandered across the Rio Grande near the ranches while searching for strayed or rustled cattle.

Residents of El Paso tried to recover the bodies from the Mexican authorities, but the buying price zoomed to seventy-five dollars for each corpse, an amount impossible to raise. Since the ransom was not soon forthcoming, the cadavers were simply rolled into the ditch and covered with dirt.

As for the other prisoners, three months later Ryan,

Davis, and Allen again broke out of the Mexican jail and this time made it without incident to the American side of the river. Hugh Cox was too ill to run and thus became the only prisoner left from that ill-fated night of January 28. In September of that year, he obtained a medical certificate and was released.[6]

So this was the situation when Dallas Stoudenmire became city marshal. Hostile eyes glared back and forth across the Rio Grande. More blood would soon be shed and the fortunes of Marshal Stoudenmire would be involved.

chapter **3** STOUDENMIRE
—THE EARLY YEARS

D ALLAS STOUDENMIRE was born on December 11, 1845, in Aberfoil, Macon County,[1] Alabama. A check of the 1850 census shows his father, Lewis Stoudenmire, to have been a farmer from South Carolina. Apparently the family lived between moderate and well to do circumstances. The census listed the assets of the elder Stoudenmire at $4000.

The census listed Lewis at the advanced age of sixty-six, and his wife, Elizabeth, forty-one. The couple had nine children, all born in Alabama, the oldest being Abednego, age twenty-three. Apparently Lewis had been married before, the records indicating that he wed his present wife Elizabeth Leger (or Seger) on August 24, 1836,[2] in Pike County, Alabama.

A Biblical scholar, Lewis indicated some fondness for Old Testament names. Abednego and Meshak were christened after two of the most obscure characters in the Bible. After Abednego, the others were Meshak, 21; Morgan, 19; John M., 13; Ann Alabama, 11; Virginia M., 11; Dallas, 6; and twins, Samuel and Elizabeth, 10 months. According to the census, the three eldest children were farmers; the next three attended school.

Lewis was a direct descendant of German colonists who settled the Orangeburg district of South Carolina about 1835.[3] As the families began to spread out, many changed the Stoudenmire spelling so that numerous versions of it now exist. In addition, because of the lack of sufficient women, the clan started to intermarry. Ann Alabama Stoudenmire wed a Charles Wesley Stoudenmire—they were first cousins.[4] Also, the Stoudenmires married heavily into the Gholson family, another group of people with the habit of spelling the ancestral name several different ways.

Although there are numerous problems concerning Lewis Stoudenmire's antecedents, he is thought to be either a brother of Jacob Stoudenmire, a carpenter,[5] or John George Stoudenmire, owner of a plantation in Autauga County, Alabama. (Perhaps Lewis, Jacob, and John George were all three brothers.) At any rate, the John George mansion stood on a beautiful plateau called Dutch Bend which overlooked the Alabama River near Autaugaville.[6]

Within the next three years after 1850, Lewis lay dead of an undisclosed ailment. On June 28, 1853, his widow married Lewis Golsan (a variant of the Gholson spelling). Together they were appointed administrators of the estate of Lewis Stoudenmire.[7] Elizabeth's luck proved no better with Mr. Golsan; he died on September 24, 1856.[8] In 1860 the Pike County, Alabama, census lists her as a widow residing with her three smallest children, Dallas, Samuel, and Elizabeth.

Apparently the other children were busily fending for themselves. Virginia was nineteen and married to I. C. B. May as of October 27, 1859.[9] Later May would die or they would be divorced and she would stick close to brother Dallas to be with him through all his troubles in El Paso. Abednego married Mary Ann Billingsley on May 14, 1853,[10] and may have provided for some of his brothers and sisters; the Gholsons had done likewise. Both clans were known to care for homeless waifs.[11]

In 1862, with the Civil War adding strain to deteriorating family relationships, Dallas Stoudenmire left his mother and without permission enlisted as a private in the Confederate Army. He looked older than his sixteen years and had no trouble fooling the enlistment officers. His papers, signed at Fort Deposit, Alabama, indicate only that he intended to fight for three years or the duration of the war. An officer of Company E, 45th Alabama Infantry Regiment, swore him in.[12]

Dallas Stoudenmire's first experience with army life proved to be short. On February 10, 1863, while he was stationed near Tullahoma, Tennessee, a message signed by General Bragg arrived at headquarters: "Private Stoudenmire . . . being under age . . . is hereby discharged from the service of the Confederate States."

Dallas grabbed his discharge and hurried south to Alabama. One month later, on March 15, he reenlisted in Company B, 6th Regiment of the Alabama Cavalry. Scratching out his signature at Troy, Alabama, he once again gave his pledge to fight for the remainder of the war.

This time the "duration" was seven months. His sins, whatever they were, found him out and he received a discharge on October 31.

It was five months before he reenlisted on March 8, 1864, joining Company F of the 17th Regiment of Alabama Volunteers.[13] Enlisting at Elba, Alabama, this time he actually served for the duration of the fighting. He surrendered at Greensboro, North Carolina, with General Joe Johnston. Parole was given in accordance with terms of the military convention entered into April 12, 1865, between Johnston, commander of Confederate forces in North Carolina, and Major General William Tecumseh Sherman, commanding officer of the United States Army in North Carolina.[14]

Later in El Paso, Stoudenmire would speak of being wounded severely four times, and unable to count the number of small wounds he had received in combat.[15] An eye-witness account was later to confirm much of this. Shortly before Dallas Stoudenmire's death, he was bathing at the hot springs in what is now Truth or Consequences, New Mexico. There a startled attendant noted that Stoudenmire's body "bears the scars of twenty-seven wounds and three bullets are still in his body."[16]

If Stoudenmire's war record is judged by the fearlessness he exhibited while serving as the El Paso City Marshal, it is easy to see how he might have been wounded in action. The wonder is that he survived at all.

After the surrender, he found himself in a ruined land. With a bleak past behind him and an uncertain future in front, he did what many other young men were doing. He went west.

Immediately after the war, brother Abednego left for Upshur County, Texas, with his wife's relatives.[17] Dallas undoubtedly went along since he showed up at about the same time at a German colony farther south in Colorado County. A brother was with Dallas, one whose name is presently unknown. The residents spoke of this brother respectfully as Colonel Stoudenmire and remember him as being older than Dallas, somber and dignified. In addition, the Colonel sported a long flowing beard.[18]

There is more than the shadow of a possibility that Dallas appeared in one of the Confederate colonies in Mexico. A relative, George Milton, spent some time in Cordoba, Mexico, lost a child there, and was finally driven out by the *Juaristas* after the fall of Maximilian.[19] It is interesting to note that Doc Manning, who was to become one of Stoudenmire's bitterest enemies in El Paso, also reportedly sold his guns to Maximilian and was forced to leave the country after the Frenchman was slain.[20]

According to his own story, Dallas settled near Columbus in Colorado County, Texas, and farmed in 1867. For several years he must have lived and roamed about in that vicinity. No account of his life during this period has filtered down through the decades (a strong hint that he may have been in Mexico at least on occasions).

On January 17, 1874, Dallas enlisted as a Second Sergeant in Captain J. R. Waller's Company A of Texas Rangers.[21] A lone letter in the Texas University Archives records some of this group's duties—none of their accomplishments. It notes that Captain Waller's company would "patrol near the western corner of Erath County and north to Stevens County and southwest to Brown County." The unit was regularly stationed in Comanche County.[22]

The primary purpose of these rangers was Indian fighting, the letter continuing with "keep an accurate account of all [Indian] depredations, number of settlers killed or carried off, amount of property recaptured, number of Indians killed, and distances traveled."

Although a sergeant's rating was nothing to sneer

about, Dallas boasted to the El Paso newspapers that he had achieved the rank of lieutenant. Probably he shaved the truth here, but such an appointment was not an impossibility. Perhaps he did serve as a lieutenant on a temporary basis.

After the Civil War, the State of Texas found itself nearly bankrupt and with very little money for law enforcement. So ranger organizing never occurred until a crisis arose. When the trouble dissolved, the rangers were disbanded and everyone went home. On February 17, Company A suffered a disbandment until May when Captain Waller reactivated his company and Stoudenmire reentered as a private.

Like most of the Southern states, Texas reeled financially during the 1870s. Rangers were called into service on a moment's notice and discharged the same way. Pay and rations were meager or nonexistent. Even firearms were difficult to come by. Strict accounting was made of all that were issued. When a service weapon disappeared, the cost was promptly deducted from a ranger's wages. Records note that Dallas Stoudenmire was furnished with a rifle. He owned a revolver.

On September 20 Captain Waller resigned; he could no longer tolerate the Texas government's methods of subsidizing the ranger efforts. Major Jones, commander of the ranger forces in the field, said, "I find much dissatisfaction and disposition to quit and go home among men on the whole line because of not being paid. Many have debts, mothers, sisters, expecting money to be sent."[23]

Dallas, who gave his occupation as a carpenter, received a discharge again on August 25. Reenlisting the same day, he accepted a discharge for the final time on December 15. Mustering-out pay came to exactly ten dollars.[24] He stuck the money in his pocket and rode away without looking back.

Stoudenmire drifted over to Colorado County and paused at the German settlement of Mentz, near Alleyton. Here he became a wheelwright and a public-spirited citizen.

On September 14, 1876, he sat on a jury and heard charges brought against an outhouse for being a nauseating annoyance. The privy was duly represented by an attorney, and after the arguments in the case had been given, the jury retired to render the following verdict: "We the jury find the privy a public nuisance and order the proper authorities to have it cleaned."[25]

In addition to his efforts to sanitize Colorado County, Dallas Stoudenmire began to secure his first solid foothold as a gunslinger.

Alleyton and Mentz were full of big, normally goodnatured, but hard-drinking and lusty-living German Americans—all of whom took little nonsense from their neighbors and even less from each other.

In no time at all, Dallas had established a reputation as one who loved the sporting life. Tales are still repeated (most of them distorted and exaggerated by time) of how he liked to drink, fight, and hurrah with the boys. Besides women, some of his other loves were the horse races and dog fights. He is reputed to have trained a stallion to attack on command, biting adversaries on the leg.[26]

For him the countryside seemed full of two different types of people, friends and enemies. Some old time residents of Alleyton still recall how their parents and other relatives spoke of the tall gunman. "He was a man who laughed a lot," one person commented. "And what he said made others laugh too."[27]

Naturally, a man of Stoudenmire's personality found an abundance of antagonists. Soon a large number of feuds developed— it being well to keep in mind that during the 1870s, feuds were as natural and normal as Texas sunshine.

C. L. Sonnichsen, the Southwest's best-known feud authority, remarks in his book *I'll Die Before I'll Run* that "feud troubles occur, usually . . . among the conservative people who cling to their ancient folkways. Strictly speaking, such people are not lawless— they are just operating under an earlier and more primitive code."[28]

One tale about Stoudenmire concerns a gunfight with an unidentified gunman. The nature of the trouble is obscure, but both men had been nursing a bitter grudge for several months and one morning met by accident (so it is said) while each rode alone on the Bernardo Prairie. Both just happened to be heavily armed and praying for trouble. The gladiators immediately dismounted, exchanged insults, and threw down their challenge.

Circling each other warily, they fired an occasional

long-range shot from their pistols. None of the balls took effect. All the while they drew closer, until finally Dallas, being the better marksman, shot his opponent down and watched him die.[29]

On another occasion, Dallas attended a party with about fifty Germans. For reasons which he never bothered to reveal, an argument developed and turned into a brawl. While Stoudenmire did manage to shoot and wound several of his opponents, he himself was wounded, captured, had his hands tied behind his back. A chain bound his ankles securely to a gin-house lever. Taking no chances, the Germans placed a guard over their prisoner.

As the hours passed, the sentinel grew careless or dropped into a drunken slumber, not noticing that Dallas had managed to free his hands and obtain a double-barreled shotgun. A few minutes later the guard was in a bound position and Dallas sprang free. Days later, a grand jury convened to investigate the incident, but passed down no indictments.[30]

Other troubles were not far ahead. Dallas and a friend named Tuck Hoover, plus a few other men who could be counted on to handle a gun, had a falling out with the Sparks boys, a clannish group of ranching brothers who lived below Eagle Lake, Texas. A dispute over open-range cattle started the difficulties; both sides claimed ownership of the beeves and a showdown developed. It ended in a flurry of killings, two bodies being brought back to Alleyton in a buckboard. Dead were Benton Duke and his son "Little Duke," associates of the Sparks brothers. One Sparks was also seriously wounded but recovered.[31]

Stoudenmire had his enemies; he also had his loyal friends. Two of his best were Buck and Tuck Hoover, brothers who, like Dallas, were quick to laugh or fight. Tuck's fortune took a sour twist; he was slain about 1894,[32] many years after Dallas Stoudenmire had established a reputation in El Paso, Texas. Tuck had killed a saloon owner named Burtshell and walked around out of jail on bond. While strolling down Alleyton's mainstreet, he was gunned down by Jim Coleman, a young gunman who, according to Sonnichsen, had a nasty habit of bushwhacking people.[33]

Stoudenmire and the Hoover brothers spent considerable time together. All enjoyed dancing and since Buck was a left-handed fiddle player in constant demand at parties, the three traveled together about the territory. Sometimes they rode more than forty miles so Buck could play a single engagement.

A rakish individual who never suffered from shyness, Dallas Stoudenmire did not hesitate to ask any girl out onto the floor. Mrs. Clapp told her son in later years that Dallas had once asked her to dance.

She wanted to oblige, but was embarrassed. Blushing, she stammered, "I'm sorry, but I refuse to dance with any man who wears his pants in his boots."

"Why not?" Dallas shot right back. "I'd dance with you if your pants were in your boots."[34]

For Dallas Stoudenmire, these must have been the days of beer and bluebonnets. Yet for "health reasons" he suddenly found it advisable to visit the Texas Panhandle where, in what was then Wheeler but later became Oldham County, he and Samuel M. "Doc" Cummings operated a sheep ranch.

Sometime later (at least by 1880 according to his own chronology of events), Stoudenmire migrated to Llano County and engaged in the merchandising business. Here he had a "serious difficulty," whatever that is supposed to mean.[35]

Whatever it was, it proved serious enough for him to travel toward San Antonio and consult the highly respected Dr. John Herff, a twenty-nine-year-old physician who, born in Texas, was of Bavarian descent.[36] An intriguing fact about Dr. Herff is that he drew frequent mentions in the Colorado County *Citizen* during the 1870s, leading to the possibility that he and Stoudenmire might have known each other prior to their meeting in San Antonio.

If Dr. Herff ever kept any records, they have not been found. So it is impossible to know what ailment induced Dallas Stoudenmire to seek his services. Herff was a general practitioner, however, who treated everything from gunshot wounds to highly contagious disesase.[37]

Now the trail of Dallas Stoudenmire disappears until he arrives in El Paso and accepts the position of town marshal on April 11, 1881. Tales are told that he came up from Dallas—or that he came down from New Mexico. His own story is that he left San Antonio and came west to El Paso. Apparently he was no stranger in San Antonio, for upon his death an article printed in the San Antonio *Express* said that "Stoudenmire was well known in this city."[38] A check of that county's 1880 census fails to find a mention of him.

All of this brings up an important point. Many Texas towns were familiar haunts to the tall, imposing figure of Dallas Stoudenmire. He was a man of some notoriety; enough notoriety to readily gain the position of marshal in El Paso—a town blessed with more than its share of hard cases. That Stoudenmire's pistol had cracked in other places was indicated in his concluding remarks made for an El Paso newspaper interview: "I have had a number of serious difficulties in my life. They would make a romance of Big Foot Wallace, but my troubles have always been on the side of law and order. . . ." He characterized his mistakes as those of the head, "not of the heart."[39]

There are two versions of how Dallas Stoudenmire came to be called for the task of city marshal. One says that Mayor pro-tem Joseph Magoffin asked him to come after learning of his fearsome reputation.[40] Another is that Major Noyes Rand of El Paso spoke for him.[41]

Stoudenmire's first opposition came from the city council. At least one of the city's fathers did not act pleased by the appointment. James Hague cast an objection on the ground that Stoudenmire's $500 bond had substantial defects therein."[42] The minutes do not give any explanation.

This was Marshal Stoudenmire's first round of trouble with the city council. His difficulties with these men and the aldermen who succeeded them were to continue for the remainder of his career.

The new marshal's appointment gained endorsement, and the resignation of William Johnson was accepted. A good bet is that Johnson was completely unaware that he was about to resign.

Marshal Stoudenmire's first act was to inform Johnson that a change had been made in the department. Johnson was located at the corner of El Paso and San Antonio Streets, an intersection only a whiskey glass away from Frank Manning's saloon.

"Johnson," Dallas snapped. "I want the keys to the jail."

Johnson had a little trouble understanding what was happening. Slowly and awkwardly he pulled a ring from his pocket holding two keys looking exactly alike. "One of these belongs to my stable." he muttered. "I will go home soon and see which is the right one and bring it to you."

"Damn you, I want them now!" Stoudenmire snarled, and he grabbed the ex-marshal, shook him violently and tore the ring from his hand.

A pathetic Johnson stood there reeling, waiting for his alcoholic fog to lift, and watching the new marshal stomp away with the keys. Johnson wasn't certain what he should do—his mental processes simply took a long time to function.

Texas Ranger Frank Beaumont was observing the incident. He approached Johnson, took him gently by the arm, and cautioned him to go home and sober up.[43]

Johnson went home, but from that minute forward the enemies of Dallas Stoudenmire never forgot what the marshal had done to Bill's pride. They plied him with whiskey and urged him to seek revenge. As far as is known, Johnson never drew a sober breath until a week later when he tried to assassinate Dallas Stoudenmire and was himself shot dead in the city street.

chapter **4** FOUR DEAD MEN
IN FIVE SECONDS

DALLAS STOUDENMIRE'S first act as city marshal was to take a slow stroll through the center of town. Obviously he wanted to see El Paso and more importantly he wanted El Paso to see him.

There was very little brick and not a single frame building to be seen. The dreary, rock-hard, mud structures leaned their sun-baked ugly fronts toward the streets which, straight and wide, differed from the buildings by being softer mixtures of caliche and sand.

There were only three streets worthy of name, the one called El Paso taking precedence as the most important and most heavily traveled. Here lay the pulsating heart of the town. To the north, El Paso Street dwindled out and disappeared near the soon-to-be constructed Southern Pacific railroad tracks. To the south, El Paso pinched down to a narrow path and meandered toward the Rio Grande and Paso del Norte, Mexico, about a mile beyond. Near the lower portion of El Paso Street, Overland intersected. Overland was the town's favorite place to hold horseraces. In addition to being straight and level, it was handy to the saloons where the races were hatched and the bets were collected. A block north and running parallel to Overland lay San Antonio Street, a dusty, cottonwood-lined trail which ended fifteen miles distant in Ysleta.

The town was quiet except for the plop of Dallas Stoudenmire's boots in the dust. His shadow flitted darkly against the whitewashed adobe pillars, huge three-foot-square supports straining under the continuous line of projecting roofs. Except for a few wind-stung trees, these galleries provided the only shade.

The rangers reported that during the year 1881 more continuous rain fell than had fallen during the last twenty-five.[1] So here and there Dallas skirted a mudhole. When he got his feet muddy, a few snickers flitted about inside the saloons, but no outright laughter. From all accounts, the day hung quiet.

The tall man with the granite looking chin cast a long shadow. Most of the bully-boys stayed inside, suspecting that wherever that dark cloud fell, hard times were going to follow for men in their profession. Killers and ne'er-do-wells peered over the bat-wing doors and wondered about their future. Even now they were appearing fearful, a sensation few of them were used to.

Everyone had questions about the new marshal. Was he honest? Or would he use his office to milk the merchants and crooked card dealers? Was he as intrepid as he looked? Could he be bought? How smart was he? And above all, the overriding question— how good was he with those heavy guns shoved into leather holders on his hips?[2]

Although part of the hard faction had been obliterated and buried after the brief gunfight nearly three months before in Paso del Norte, El Paso still contained a large and vicious assortment of gunmen who hung around the saloons and brothels. One moment they could be seen crossing the road, leaning against an adobe pillar while hitching up a sagging gunbelt, or entering one of the gambling establishments. The next moment they would be gone, only a wisp of dust floating in the hazy sky to indicate where a horse had been ridden. Sometimes the men wouldn't come back, disappearing forever with little trace or evidence that they had passed this way. Other times they would reappear, their pockets bulging with money which everyone knew they had obtained without sweat or blisters. Of course, the bankrolls usually vanished quickly. Gamblers and girls were always contesting each other in one of the many emporiums and cribs open to relieve such people of their surplus cash.

Stoudenmire knew of the eyes behind the saloon doors and of the gunmen. He had pieced the story together from Ranger Captain George Baylor and the others. Baylor knew where these gunmen had obtained their money. And he also knew that there was nothing he could do about it.

"All of the horse thieves, murderers, and rowdies that the rangers have run out of Texas in the last five years are congregated in the . . . corner of New Mexico and are so strong and defiant that New Mexico cannot oust them. They have been raiding into Mexico, driving off hundreds of head of cattle and horses."

But Baylor could boast on at least one score. Had it not been for him and his rangers, the outlaws "would have carried on the holding-up business here and made El Paso their headquarters."[3]

The dark, forbidding *bosques*, swamps and thickets lining the Rio Grande like a chain of thorns, provided the perfect hiding place near Marshal Stoudenmire's domain. There were two portions, the upper and lower *bosque*. Newspapers told of screams coming from them at night. The marshy land, the bogs, the cattails, the saber-like grasses loomed so impenetrable that only those outlaws familiar with the narrow, winding paths and trails dared traverse them. Some of the most savage and merciless gangs ever to infest the Southwest took cover here. Primarily they were dedicated to stealing livestock, although anyone ignorant enough to wander into the jungle was apt to pay for his carelessness with both his money and his life.

Examination of a dead man proved futile. When a body did turn up, witnesses—if any—were too frightened to testify.

Men on the dodge moved freely from one *bosque* to the other. Those not wanting to be observed followed the river's course. Stock could not be transported this way, of course. Even the cattle hesitated about allowing themselves to be driven into what could be bottomless sand. If stolen animals were needed in the upper *bosque*, the rustlers drove them across the mesa, the high, flat, mesquite and cactus covered desert plain on the northeast side of El Paso. From there the cattle were pushed across the Franklin Mountains. Outlaw hordes regularly swept over the mountain passes without any particular fear of being trailed. The terrain was so rocky and hard that only an expert could tell that cattle once passed that way. One gap saw such frequent use that it became familarly known as Smugglers Pass. Corrals were built on the western slopes.[4]

The lower *bosque* was the largest. Sprawling out to the east of El Paso, it became a green island about ten miles in length and one mile broad at its widest point. An early shifting of the Rio Grande bed brought about this condition, and its steaming thickets extended completely past Ysleta.

The upper *bosque* harbored most of the stolen Mexican cattle. This swamp was somewhat smaller than the lower one, and was tucked neatly into the corner of Texas and the Territory of New Mexico, with old Mexico lying directly to the south. Communications between law officers in the three areas were sparse and erratic because of distance and the difficulties of fast travel. All three sides could never get together and conduct a thorough search.

Some of the Southwest's toughest hard-cases had ranches here, the homes being little more than huts camouflaged among briars and cottonwoods. Baylor once noted that in the big cottonwood trees, a careful eye could oftentimes spot platforms built among the thick branches and leaves.[5] A thief could comfortably take a nap while waiting for a posse to end its futile search and drift on its way. Or, in some cases, if the searchers were composed of only a man or two, a shotgun blast had the quick effect of setting the rustler's mind to rest. James Gillett referred to these outlaws as the Canutillo Gang.[6]

Three brothers were principally responsible for much of the rustling and banditry that was so rampart in the upper *bosque*. James, John, and Frank Manning owned a small ranch near Canutillo, a spread which George Baylor described as the outlaw "base of operations."[7] Another brother, George Felix "Doc" Manning, was soon to appear on the scene and make his influence felt. But by that time the Manning rustling empire would have crumbled beneath the two smoking guns of Dallas Stoudenmire.

Adjacent to the Manning ranch was the eighty-acre property of John Hale, a worthless section of swamp. Hale was a husky, thirty-six-year-old Iowan, the only man in the locality who could gaze down at Dallas Stoudenmire. With his parents, who were English, he migrated to California early in life and then moved to El Paso as a fighting member of Carleton's California Column.[8] His career is little known; he stepped into historical focus only long enough to die.

Rangers often swooped down on the Hale and Manning ranches. However, these forays rarely turned up any quarry. Spies had so thoroughly infiltrated Captain Baylor's company that most of the bandits were warned hours in advance when a strike was about to be fashioned.

Some of the gunmen identified with the firm of Manning and Hale were Frank Stevenson, Chris Peveler, T. L. Weldon, and George Campbell.

Frank Stevenson was unquestionably the most notorious member of the gang. He was crippled in his right hand and had a matching intellect. Baylor described him as a liar, assassin, and thief, run out of Hays County after killing a farmer who caught him stealing hogs. Frank then migrated to Seven Rivers, New Mexico (a few years later to be the scene of rustling and rampaging operations by Jesse Evans and John Selman),[9] where under the *alias* of Will Wallace, in league with a man named Goode, he began an early and short-lived venture in rustling John Chisum's cattle. This nefarious enterprise ended when Goode stopped a bullet and retired to the cemetery.[10]

For health reasons Stevenson started running for the Rio Grande where he teamed up with the others, especially with Chris Peveler, *alias* Lum (or Lem) Peterson. Peveler was a former Texas Ranger who doubled on the side as a cattle thief.[11] Together these four men were the backbone of lawlessness in the upper *bosque*, although Campbell confined much of his attention to brooding over the injustice of being out of a job.

Shortly after the charges of attempted murder and shooting up the town of El Paso were dropped, George Campbell rode in to look the new marshal over. He found Stoudenmire finishing his downtown stroll. Unawed by the Marshal's reputation, George boasted that he would "try him on before five days."[12]

. . . .

On April 12, 1881, the day after Dallas Stoudenmire was appointed city marshal, the *jefe politico*[13] of Paso del Norte, Don Ynocente Ochoa, approached Captain Baylor and complained that thirty head of his cattle had been rustled from his ranch thirty-five miles south of the border. The trail led directly to Johnny Hale's corrals.[14] Snorting with anger, Senor Ochoa placed the matter directly in Baylor's hands and demanded that the rangers do something.

This was a tricky assignment for Baylor. He already knew the futility of raiding the Hale ranch and besides, most of his rangers were on assignment elsewhere. He himself would not go. Gillett said Baylor perferred chasing Indians and generally dispatched other men to the outlaw trail.[15] Private Ed Fitch rode in from patrol at this minute and received an assignment to recover the stock and apprehend the rustlers. Eight Mexican nationals went with the ranger. Then *jefe* said they could identify the steers.

As an afterthought, two others, Juarique and Sanchez, decided to tag along and they hurried to catch up with the main force. One of these Mexicans was reportedly the rifleman who slew Thompson, O'Neal, and Cain in the irrigation ditch in February.

At Hale's ranch a vigorous argument developed between the posse and the alleged rustlers. Only three head of Ochoa's branded cattle were found and Johnny Hale snarled that he had purchased these from the owner. At this point the ranger and his assistants turned to go back, all except Juarique and Sanchez who decided to split off and search the thickets for the remainder of the cattle. Hale and his companions merely smiled grimly at this; in their minds both *vaqueros* were marked for death.

Juarique and Sanchez were the first to die in the bloody episode of slaughter. Ex-ranger Chris Peveler and Frank Stevenson trailed the boys, slipping silently behind them, getting ever closer until the opportunity arrived to spring the ambush. Both Mexicans slumped under a barrage of rifle fire. From a short distance away, T. L. Weldon and John Hale witnessed the massacre. When the killing had first been agreed upon, Weldon and Hale planned to assist. After some second thoughts, however, they thought it best to stay behind and act as witnesses. They would swear that the Mexican youths had attacked first and Stevenson and Peveler did little more than defend themselves.

The 12th and the 13th of April passed and the two Mexicans did not return. On the morning of the 14th, a party of heavily armed Mexicans (George Look says seventy-five or eighty strong) crossed into Texas and asked Gus Krempkau, an honest man who rode west with Captain Baylor in 1879 but was now believed to be an El Paso constable, to lead them in an attempt to recover the bodies. Krempkau complied.

Alderman Warren Phillips also went along. He later testified at the inquest that "it was plain to him that the young Mexicans had stopped under a shade tree to eat and smoke and their assailants had crept up and killed them both."[16]

Private Fitch had an idea who the murderers were. As the posse headed for the upper *bosque*, Fitch cut out for Hale's ranch, where he arrested Peveler and Stevenson, brought them into town, charged them with murder, and placed them under bond with orders to show up when a hearing was ordered.

At the first light of dawn, the posse found the boys and loaded them on buckboards for transportation back to town. Arriving at about ten or eleven o'clock in the morning, the riders resembled a party of war and were in a hostile and threatening mood. The procession stopped at the office of Judge Buckler on the west side of El Paso Street, the first door down from the present day corner of West San Antonio Street. On the north side and next to the Judge's office stood Paul Keating's Saloon, and only a half dozen doors away was Frank Manning's Saloon. Across the street from Buckler was merchant Ben Schuster's store.

Judge Buckler took one look at the bullet-saturated bodies and agreed that an inquest was necessary. He started immediately.

It was common knowlege that Stevenson and Peveler were the slayers; they were accused right away. Gus Krempkau argued actively to get both men indicted for murder. The assassins, however, were conveniently absent. Only Hale and Weldon were present, two "eye witnesses" defending their friends from "false accusations." Also in attendance sat ex-marshal George Campbell, who naturally supported the right side.

So far no trouble between the Mexican and American factions had broken out. Nevertheless, each party stood nervously grouped along the street, muttering threats and staying close to their guns. In particular, the Mexicans were upset over the miscarriage of justice which, they felt, was about to be perpetrated.

Helping the tension along were the occasional snarls, yells, and curses, both in Spanish and English, that carried through the adobe walls of the judge's office and echoed along El Paso Street. Only Buckler's foresight in insisting that everyone park their guns next door in Keating's Saloon prevented a blood-letting from happening in his office.

Ben Schuster, a respected merchant and member of the city council, tried to persuade both parties in the streets to disarm and tone down their threats. When his pleas aroused no response, he caught G. F. Neill, the prosecuting attorney, by the arm and pointed out the situation. Neill quickly terminated the inquest and the fuse fizzled as the bodies were ferried across the Rio Grande to Mexican soil.

Marshal Stoudenmire relaxed as the Mexicans drifted across the river. Shoving his hands in his pockets, he strolled across the street toward the Globe Restaurant and a late lunch.[18]

This left Constable Gus Krempkau alone to face his hostile neighbors. While the hearing had been in progress, Gus had been relatively safe from attack. He now went next door to pick up his rifle and gun belt.

Outside in the sand of El Paso Street, Gus could hear George Campbell, heavily fortified with drink, yelling that the Mexicans ought to be arrested for riding armed in El Paso. "Where's our new marshal, Stoudenmire?" he asked sourly. At the same time he glanced belligerently around as if daring Stoudenmire to enforce the law.

And then Krempkau was in the street, standing beside his riding mule, sliding the rifle into the scabbard. The sight of Gus striding outside only further aggravated Campbell's alcoholic bellicosity. "Any American that is a friend of Mexicans ought to be hanged!"

Krempkau turned red. He faced the ex-marshal. "George, I hope you don't mean me," his voice cracked out.

"If the shoe fits, wear it," Campbell hooted and

snapped his fingers in the air.

This was evidently as far as George Campbell intended to carry the conversation or the dispute. He turned and stomped away, reaching for the reins of his own mule.

John Hale, who had been sitting in a window right near the door of Keating's Saloon, was also under the influence. He jumped up and shoved a heavy forty-five beneath Campbell's arm which was upraised and in the process of untying his mount's reins from a tree limb.

"Turn loose, Campbell. I've got him covered," Hale yelled. At the same instant he fired. Krampkau reeled as the ball struck near his heart, tearing an exit through the lungs. His right hand pulled his revolver free as he fell.

From across the street, Dallas threw open the restaurant door, and pulling his guns, jumped outside. Close behind came Doc Cummings with a shotgun.

Stoudenmire's first shot roared as Hale jumped behind an adobe pillar supporting the saloon roof. However, the Marshal's running gait caused the bullet to whistle past the intended victim's shoulder and thump into an innocent Mexican named Lopez or Ochoa. The bystander had been quietly minding his own business and purchasing a sack of peanuts from Charlie Lawrence. At Hale's shot, he turned and began racing the length of the street for cover, but he crossed in front of the Marshal's gunsight and a bullet entered his back. He died the next morning.[19]

Undaunted by his bad aim, Stoudenmire never paused in his shooting. As Johnny Hale peered from behind the pillar, Dallas sent a bullet exploding in his brain. The rustler collapsed, instantly dead.

Campbell watched incredulously as Hale folded up. Earlier whiskey had made George a tough talker; now he appeared badly frightened and his courage and pugnaciousness rapidly oozed away. Fear made him commit an almost unbelievable act. Backing hastily into the street, he pulled his pistol. Swinging it back and forth as if he were trying to cover everyone, he shouted "Gentlemen, this is not my fight."[20]

George Campbell found himself in developments he

could no longer control. Gus Krempkau, dying and sagging against the saloon door casing, weakly managed to pull his revolver as he slid slowly to the ground. Turning toward Campbell, whom he may have blamed for shooting him, he gritted his teeth and one by one began squeezing off shots from his pistol.

The first slug smashed Campbell's pistol from his right hand and broke his wrist. George screamed and scooped the gun up from the street with his left hand. Krempkau was still shooting. One of the bullets struck Campbell in the foot. The others buried themselves in adobe walls as onlookers cleared the streets.

In the meantime, Stoudenmire turned from the dead Hale and began firing at Campbell, who was struggling and cursing along in an effort to escape. Many people, including several rangers, had heard George shout that he did not wish to become involved—they did little but stand there. Whether Stoudenmire heard will have to be judged by a higher power. It bears remembering that here stood an armed man who had recently threatened the marshal.

Stoudenmire whirled and saw a dangerous adversary with a gun. One did not listen to pleas under such circumstances; it was enough that an enemy faced him with a gun and he did exactly what any sensible marshal would have done. He sent a bullet crashing into Campbell's body.

George dropped his gun, grabbed his stomach, and toppled on his face. He knew he lay dying. Rolling over, he looked up at Stoudenmire and gasped, "You big son-of-a-bitch, you murdered me."[21]

Whether or not he was murdered might be subject to dispute. The fact that his career was over seemed a certainty. Two men picked him up by the arms and legs and carried him to the Overland Building, where he died the following day.

As Campbell lay in his own blood on El Paso Street, Pat Shea, a tough friend of the ex-marshal, saw instantly that his partner was dying. Pat had always admired George's revolver. Figuring that his friend might pass away at any moment and the weapon would be lost to him forever, Pat ran up and yelled, "George, do you want your gun?"

Stoudenmire intercepted the questioner quickly.

Ramming his two guns under the nose of Shea, he gave Pat a good sniff of the still smoking barrels. As Shea backed away, George Look walked over, picked up the weapon and gave it to Vanston, the bartender at Keating's Saloon. About two o'clock that night, Campbell sent for Look, asked where his gun was, and requested that it be given to Shea.[22]

An El Paso grocer named Zach White also hurried to the scene of the shooting. He was anxious to see who lay on the ground, perhaps fearing that he had lost a customer. This time Stoudenmire did not bother to pull his guns. He stopped White with a string of profanity that knocked him backwards across the street. As White moved toward his store, he noticed an Irish employee hiding behind one of the adobe gallery supports. Wiping the sweat from his forehead, he stammered, "This damn post is too small to hide a man in such a battle."[23,24]

As for Chris Peveler and Frank Stevenson, they were riding into town to attend the inquest as the shooting broke out. Just as they started down El Paso Street, Hale fell with a bullet in his head. Not wanting any part of this, they hurriedly spun their horses and galloped back to the Manning Ranch after which they slipped back and forth across the New Mexico territorial line.

Baylor made out a warrant for their arrest and Gillett set out to serve it. In doing so, he crossed the State line, explaining, "This was prior to the Government orders and Laws of Texas reaching me."

Peveler and Stevenson were not captured. They sent a threatening message to Baylor and Sergeant Gillett. According to the ranger captain, the note read that "they [the outlaws] had plenty of guns and several thousand rounds of ammunition and intended to shell me [Baylor] the first time I came after them, and . . . they wanted their friends among the rangers to stand aside as they did not wish to hurt them."[25]

Messages like this infuriated Baylor and Gillett as well as the other rangers. On June 7, Captain Baylor with eight men camped at Mundy's Ranch on the east side of the Franklin Mountains. Early the next morning, they crossed through the passes and spent all day searching for the fugitives along the Rio Grande. The gunmen had been warned, however, and had fled to New Mexico.

On June 12, Sergeant Gillett made an unsuccessful search along the river, gaining little except some information. This knowledge brought him back with six men on the 16th of June. They camped near the Canutillo road leading to El Paso; rumor had it that Peveler, Stevenson, and another wanted man named Smith would travel that way. All day long the rangers patiently waited, and when night fell they were rewarded by the sound of horses hooves on the hard-packed dirt.

"Hands up!" Gillett shouted but he might just as well have shouted orders to the fish in the river. The night loomed pitch black and the horsemen, upon being halted, immediately rammed spurs to their mounts and ran. Firing thirty-two rounds of ammunition at the escapees, the rangers managed to shoot one horse and capture a hat. The gunmen escaped.[26]

Even fugitives can get tired of running and they did not wish to remain forever in New Mexico. Although often seen in the vicinity of Las Cruces and San Augustin, New Mexico,[27] the boys' hearts were still in Texas. So when word reached them that their return would be looked upon favorably in El Paso, they rode in, were "examined" by a justice of the peace (a Dogberry according to Baylor), and were released.[28]

Peveler and Stevenson had no sooner been turned loose than a complaint was lodged against them by the Mexican authorities. The charge was the usual one—rustling cattle. This time thirteen head had been stolen and driven across the Rio Grande. Baylor picked up a warrant and went after them.

With six rangers and several Mexican guides, the captain followed a dim trail all day and then camped that night in a bend of the Rio Grande. The next morning both the rustlers and the cattle were located, but unfortunately Baylor was spotted by some Mexican rustling associates from the other bank. Shots were fired as a signal to the outlaws on the American side. Instantly the cattle were driven back across the Rio Grande onto Mexican soil. This removed the matter from ranger jurisdiction, so Baylor took his men back to camp.

On the following day Chris Peveler walked into the ranger camp and complained to Baylor that the Mexican guides who were employed by the rangers had stolen his horses. Two friends, ranger privates Bond and Bassett, accompanied Chris into the compound. Peveler's complaint was rejected; instead Baylor and Gillett got together and questioned Peveler about the threatening note they had received some time before. Chris began to bluster, so Gillett grabbed a Winchester and Baylor a shotgun. Together they backed the gunman out of the camp, cussed him soundly, and warned him never to return. A still smoldering Baylor then summoned rangers Bond and Bassett into his tent and wrote out their discharges on the spot.[29]

Bond and Peveler went to Deming, New Mexico, became drunk and tried to tree the town. For amusement, Bond grabbed an old man by the arms, spun him around, and cracked his head with a six-shooter. Dan Tucker, Deming's deputy sheriff, came on the run with a double-barreled shotgun. The first barrel sent Bond sprawling dead in the street. Peveler screamed and shoved both hands into the air just as Tucker unloaded the second barrel. Fortunately, the deputy twisted his gun aside at the last second and the buckshot buried itself in the wall, narrowly missing Peveler.[30]

Back in El Paso, Chris Peveler and Frank Stevenson stole Judge Magoffin's carriage horses. Stevenson was later captured by Gillett and received fifteen years in prison for his rustling ways.[31] Peveler dropped from sight.

As for Dallas Stoudenmire, a coroner's jury came hastily into action and rendered the following verdict: "We the jury agree that Gus Krempkau came to his death by a pistol shot fired by John Hale, and Campbell and John Hale came to their deaths by pistol shots fired by City Marshal Dallas Stoudenmire in executing his duties as Marshal for the city of El Paso."[32]

Conveniently overlooked was the innocent Mexican who had been slain. However, nothing could be done about it. Section 97 of the City Act of Incorporation stated: "No officer shall be liable for damages for any act committed in the proper discharge of his duties."

The city of El Paso gave Dallas Stoudenmire a gold headed cane in appreciation of his fine work.

As a footnote to the battle, John Hale proved to be too tall in death. No coffin could be found large enough to contain him. His family had to accept what was available, so the undertaker took the largest casket he had and stuffed the gunman inside like wadding in a shotgun. His knees were propped up with pillows in order to fit his length inside. Concordia Cemetery now holds his unknown and unmarked grave. His ranch passed on to his Mexican wife and became known as the Rancho Angelita.[33] With her death, the land was parceled out in bits and pieces. Today the Hale descendants live in respectable but poor and modest circumstances. The land they once prized, and still live near, is now almost beyond value and is a part of the El Paso Country Club district.

chapter **5**   ATTEMPTED ASSASSINATION

THE MANNING brothers were men of bitter hates and fierce loyalties. In many respects they were no different from Dallas Stoudenmire. This may be one reason why Stoudenmire and the brothers never got along—they were entirely too much alike. One example was the way they all felt about the South losing the Civil War. Dallas perhaps was not as dogmatic in his feelings as the Mannings, but he liked to tell tales which upgraded his fighting prowess and indicated that he stood ready to continue the struggle after the war had ended.

On the other hand, the Mannings vowed never to shave until the Confederacy had emerged victorious from defeat.[1] Each brother kept that promise, wearing at least a mustache until the day of his death.

In some respects the Mannings were leaders of the El Paso community. In 1881, James Manning even ran for mayor, although he finished last in a field of four candidates.[2] They were among the first to contribute to charity. Conversely they were the last to forgive a wrong.

They never forgave Dallas Stoudenmire for killing

John Hale and particularly George Campbell. Just how they expected the marshal to react when the bullets began to fly is a moot question. It seemed enough that two of their most trusted friends and allies lay dead. It was sufficient that their slayer still walked about, not only having no regrets about the slayings, but acting quite proud and pleased about his part in them.

If the Mannings ever had any trouble understanding their emotions concerning John Hale, they never indicated it. Possibly they would even admit that Hale had been a fool. He had started the fight, but to the Manning brothers this seemed to be no great sin. But he had not emerged on top of the struggle and this was sinful. To begin with, he had opened fire on the wrong man. If Marshal Stoudenmire had been shot down first, Hale might have won the battle and emerged the hero. Instead he had been careless and lost.

Circumstances surrounding the death of George Campbell were quite different. His killing disturbed not only the Mannings, but the Texas Rangers as well. Both parties thought Campbell had been murdered, the Manning brothers becoming the most vociferous about it. Nearly everyone had heard George scream from the middle of the street that the affair was not his fight. Then they watched in amazement as one of Marshal Stoudenmire's bullets cut him down. To nearly everyone except Stoudenmire, Campbell's stupidity in running out into the street and pulling a gun became an act of bad judgment, not one that justified his death.

Ranger Frank Beaumont, Sergeant V. M. Dampin, and Corporal Ed Fitch were present when Hale, Campbell, Krempkau, and the innocent Mexican were killed. Amazingly enough, the rangers even drew their guns and stood there within the shadow of all the participants without firing a shot. It would seem that they did not know what to do. Although they were later to criticize Stoudenmire for his actions, Dampin, who stood near the marshal, grabbed up the fallen Hale's pistol and handed it to Dallas, yelling that it looked nearly loaded in case he needed it.[3]

Later, Captain Baylor asked the three rangers why they did not give Stoudenmire more support. They unanimously replied that Campbell, in spite of his strange and erratic behavior, did not represent a threat to anyone and they did not feel justified in shooting him. Baylor merely nodded his head at this. Nevertheless, Captain Baylor was sympathetic to Stoudenmire's side of the dispute and took the marshal's part when writing General King: "He [Stoudenmire] did not hesitate about shooting him [Campbell] as soon as he saw him draw his pistol."[4]

The killings created a deep impression not only on the Mannings, but on the town as well. In anger, Dallas sent the rangers back to camp and began to clamp down on the saloon crowds. Toughs grew scared. Literally within hours the hard drinking and boisterous living began noticeably to taper off. The saloons were still full, but the boys were nursing their drinks and leaving early.

The Manning brothers decided that something had to be done. A plan was worked out to assassinate Marshal Stoudenmire.

The scheme proved simple. Whiskey-drinking Bill Johnson, the dim-witted ex-marshal and ex-assistant marshal, was still an alcoholic fixture around town. He could usually be found at Frank Manning's saloon on El Paso Street, his hand gripping a liquor bottle. His foot slid across the bar rail as soon as the establishment opened in the morning. It was still there when the saloon closed at night. For him, sobriety was an impossibility. He lived only to drink and to mutter hostile threats about Dallas Stoudenmire. This so encouraged the marshal's enemies that they prevailed upon the city administration to appoint Johnson as constable. This gave him legitimate reason to be seen carrying a shotgun around town.

Johnson was bent on personal vengeance and seemed undisturbed at the passing of Campbell and Hale. His intellect could focus on only one project at a time, anyway. He mentally still relived the events of a week before when Stoudenmire had so forcibly taken the key to the jail. The more Johnson brooded over his humiliation, the more encouragement he received from the Manning brothers. When the brothers were not appealing to his pride, they were playing on his fears. The Mannings told Johnson that Stoudenmire intended to kill him.[5]

In addition to keeping the dupe on edge with their words, the Mannings never allowed Johnson's glass to empty. While the constable drank—and babbled—and blustered—and threatened—and even wept, everyone appeared to be sympathetic. The Mannings solemnly nodded their heads and agreed that Marshal Stoudenmire had no right to trample on his self respect.

On Sunday, April 17, Dallas received an anonymous message warning him to get out of town "or be dead before another sun rises over the city."[6] In typical Stoudenmire fashion, he shrugged the threat aside.

As the sun dropped behind the New Mexico horizon, Dallas Stoudenmire started his evening routine, a custom that rarely varied. Before making his rounds, he visited his brother-in-law at the Globe Restaurant, an impressive eatery on El Paso Street, two doors down from the intersection of San Antonio, and convenient for the town's hungry citizens who yearned for better-than-ordinary meals. There Dallas consumed a few shots of hard whiskey, stopping before the liquor could blur his judgment or his shooting eye. Then he sauntered south, checking the side streets and alleys. On his way back, he paused for another drink and to consider plans for policing the upper end of town.

The menacing letter had prompted changes in the marshal's routine. When he left the Globe the second time, an extra gun hand paced at his side. Reliable Doc Cummings tagged along—and in his front pockets sagged two heavy revolvers.

The route taken by Stoudenmire and Cummings toward the ambush site at San Antonio and El Paso Street is controversial. One line of thinking indicates that the two circled around to San Antonio from the south and east, then walked west down the middle of the road toward the junction. Lights could be seen twinkling in the Manning Saloon, Irvin's Drug, a clothing store, and Mundy's Market.

The other line of thought is that the two men left the Globe and proceeded cautiously for the few steps up El Paso Street towards the intersection. But regardless of the route taken, death waited.

As Dallas and Doc approached the intersection, they concentrated their attention on the Manning Saloon. If trouble came, they expected it to originate from there. Neither gunman paid much attention to the large pile of bricks in front of the newly constructed State National Bank. On top of this sat Bill Johnson, his form blending in with the shadows of the building. A shotgun lay cradled in his lap, a bottle of whiskey clung to his fingers. In the mind of Johnson appeared the image of Dallas Stoudenmire's body being torn by the bite of vicious buckshot.

Suddenly Johnson heard voices approaching the corner, sounds which indicated that the marshal was not alone. The gunman peered at the two dark shapes drawing near, and he rose quietly on shaking legs. The figures were approaching slowly and the suspense became more than Johnson could stand. Prematurely he jerked the shotgun to his shoulder and yanked the triggers. But the combination of darkness, too much liquor, and an unsteady footing proved disastrous. The buckshot load soared too high.

Dallas Stoudenmire and Doc Cummings never gave Johnson an opportunity to do anything further except stand there and die. The shotgun's crash had barely died away before the assassin's chest was raked by eight bullets. Down on the brick pile Bill Johnson fell, falling over on his back as one of the last bullets severed his testicles.[7]

Although Johnson lay dead, Stoudenmire and Cummings were not out of danger. From across the street in the vicinity of Frank Manning's Saloon, other potential assassins began firing a scattering of shots, trying to finish the job that Johnson had muffed.

The accuracy of these attackers proved to be less than excellent; and Stoudenmire, as usual, did the unexpected. Instead of running or taking cover, he charged straight across the street. His opponents, unnerved by all that had taken place, had no taste for a giant with this quality of courage and ability. They scattered and left the marshal in undisputed possession of the battlefield.[8]

Dallas had his wounds, however. A ricocheting bullet punctured his heel and cussing did nothing to soothe the pain.

By this time the entire male citizenry of El Paso came stumbling into El Paso Street to investigate the shooting. Ranger Frank Beaumont said that the whole town seemed to be lit up by gunfire. He thought the battle must be involving everyone in the city.

As the shooting gradually began to subside, Doc Cummings ran to the Globe and grabbed a rifle. Upon returning, he organized a vigilante committee and the initial area he intended to clean out was Frank Manning's Saloon. The excuse given was that most of the gunfire seemed to have originated from there. "Let's go kill the damn sons-of-bitches!"[9] he roared.

Certainly the saloon was searched, but if any of the Mannings were found, no harm came to them. Still, the citizens supported Doc's idea of kangaroo law enforcement and the vigilantes were an effective force for several days until they melted away from lack of suitable prospects to hang.

Stoudenmire's injured heel left him in agony. He rode to the ranger camp for a few days rest.

In the meantime, the vigilantes had reorganized as a "Law and Order League." About thirty-five men were active, but a complete list of the membership was never made public. Knowledge of this sort was worth a man's life. Nevertheless, Major Noyes Rand, who helped bring Dallas Stoudenmire to El Paso, Solomon Schutz, former mayor, and Ben Schuster, respected merchant, were known to be three of the leaders. The first meeting took place at the rear of Alderman Krakauer's retail store and, using oil lamps and candles for light, the men squatted in a crude circle and formed their plans. Many of the flinty faces, such as Doc Cummings' were as violent as the killers they hoped to eliminate. In the majority, however, they were citizens who wished to see law and order prevail.

Immediately the town toughs started to act edgy. Several found ropes tied to the door-latch of their residence, a macabre reminder that their presence might soon be requested at a lynching.

"Look here, Sol.," one gunman said to Schutz, while nervously glancing back over his shoulder, "I am not afraid of God almighty in heaven. But I am afraid of a vigilante committee, and want to know if I should leave town."[10]

This character became one of many who vanished from El Paso and took up residence in Mesilla and Deming, New Mexico.[11]

Only hours after Stoudenmire had departed, plots were hatched to eliminate a goodly portion of Johnny Doyle's saloon customers. The vigilantes had moved their headquarters to Schuster's store (just a few doors down El Paso Street from Doyle's saloon), and they conspired to slip outside after dark and assemble in the rear corrals. Then the saloon rear door would be thrown open and the room's interior raked by rifle and shotgun fire.

Ben Schuster squelched this idea as soon as he learned of it. He protested that the saloon was crowded at night with railroad hands and laborers, some of whom slept on the benches and floor. To kill these men would be unjustifiable.[12]

To combat this core of vigilantes, the opposition organized their own. No one knows who led this group, although the Mannings must have had a hand in it. The only known violence perpetrated by this man was upon Deputy Marshal Jones. He left early for duty one night and a few minutes later his room and bed were ripped asunder by several shotgun blasts. The gunman escaped and the case was never solved.[13]

On the night Johnson was killed, the gunfire had barely echoed away before Captain Baylor, Sergeant Gillett, and seven rangers swept into town. Although the scene frothed in a ferment of great excitement, very few arrests were made. But Baylor and his men remained there until April 24. At that time, Marshal Stoudenmire had recovered his health enough to resume duties. Even then, five to eight rangers were assigned to assist the marshal until law and order were restored.

chapter **6**   THE RAILROAD COMES TO TOWN

BEFORE MAY 28, 1881, hardly anyone in El Paso had ever seen a train. But now one was due. For months the Southern Pacific had been bellowing its way in from California: the workers struggling and straining, sweating and blasting, carving narrow niches in the close-grained rock, each day getting a few more rails and a few more ties closer to El Paso. Chinese coolies had shoveled their way across half a continent from San Francisco Bay. By March of 1880 they were in Tucson, Arizona . . . by June in Benson . . . and by December in Deming, New Mexico.

Originally the correct line for the Southern Pacific Railroad lay through Mexican territory at Mesilla Pass. President Pierce was not one to slow a nation's progress on account of national boundaries, however. He sent General James Gadden to speak with President Santa Anna: "The projected railroad . . . must be built by way of the Mesilla Valley because there is no other possible route. The Mexican government will be splendidly indemnified. The Valley must belong to the United States by indemnity or we will take it."

Negotiations began at once and ended with the

American government owning the land and Mexico being paid
$10,000,000.

By April of 1881, the Chinese were toiling on the
roadbed between Deming, New Mexico, and El Paso. Oddly enough, the
Chinese contribution to the West has been nearly lost to the history
books. It was their labor which gouged the space from hot, living rock
and spun the rails across the desert. It was their hands, cracked and
bleeding, which swung the hammers, drove the spikes, and carried the
crossties. Nearly 1600 had been at work between Deming and El
Paso—a sandy and rocky stretch of roughly eighty miles, all of it
bristling with rattlesnakes, Gila monsters, and hostile Indians.

At night, El Paso residents were often startled by the
wild shooting emanating from the Chinese encampment. Although the
roar helped break up some of the dreadful monotony of their lives, no
doubt exists that much of this firing represented a Southwestern
version of the Tong Wars. Later, in El Paso, they would forego shooting
each other, and hangings became a common practice in an area now
known as Washington Park.[1] But until that time, the Chinese were the
merchants' best source of ammunition sales.[2]

When the Southern Pacific did reach El Paso, it
caught nearly everyone by suprise. Black smoke suddenly jutted over El
Paso's western horizon. Lieutenant McGonegal glanced at his watch
which showed nine o'clock and wondered why the train arrived an hour
early. In haste, he wheeled a cannon into position for the salute.

Many people had been waiting since early morning,
hoping to get a first look at the steam car. Tired, hungry, and thirsty,
part of these had drifted off to Frank Manning's saloon or Johnny
Doyle's or Paul Keating's place. A few had taken the opportunity to
visit the barber shops and others lolled around the plaza. With the
asthmatic blast of the whistle, the whole town started hustling toward
the station.

Everyone surged close as the train chugged in. Steam
hissed from the cylinders. In front, the onlookers tried to back up;
those in the rear tried to close in. The steam paused and as a solid mass
the crowd surged forward. The conductor had to stop momentarily and
warn everyone away from the wheels and firebox. "Damn it, someone's
going to get killed," he yelled.

No one paid any attention. A miner tried to grab the conductor's hand. Questions screamed from every lip. Shaking his head, the conductor climbed back inside and the train eased forward once more. Oil fumes and sulphurous smoke settled over the crowd and bit into the nostrils, but did not dim the enthusiasm. Even the ladies forgot about the effects on their white finery. Then the whistle screamed long and loud; the train had reached its destination. Tiny cinders from the smoke began dropping on every head. Those who had their hands over their ears laughingly removed them to cover their hair.

Judge Magoffin caught Marshal Stoudenmire's eye in the jostling crowd and asked him to clear a path so that the executives could climb off. Dallas could hardly hear, but he understood enough to know what was expected. Easing a soldier aside here, a cowboy aside there, and a sporting lady and a gambler somewhere else, he led the judge to the station platform and opened the train door. Colonel Charles F. Crocker, President of the Southern Pacific, stuck out his hand, barely noting that the suntanned fist he received in return looked exceptionally small to belong to a gunman.[3]

At that moment Dallas said something, his voice drowned by the belated cannon's roar. Everyone cheered, those not already hoarse from doing so. The men on board began filing out.

"Was there any trouble with the Apaches on the other side of Deming," a bearded El Pasoan asked Colonel Bean.

Bean, Superintendent of the Tucson Division, caressed the watch chain that crawled across his vest, pushed back his coat to tuck his thumbs under the blue brocade, and heaved out his stomach. He pridefully looked down the length of the coach—all twenty feet of its wainscoting over iron. "My friend, we made sure that would deflect an arrow when—"

"Or any bullet," interrupted Mr. W. E. Brown, President of the Southern Development Company, who had just dismounted.

"That's right," said Bean, "bullet or arrow, the Southern Pacific is safe from Indian attack."

"Gentlemen," Magoffin spoke, "Judge Blacker is ready with his welcoming address."

Judge Blacker was an accomplished speaker. He

addressed his talk to the fellow citizens of California, Arizona, and New Mexico—but he spoke about El Paso. "Here surrounded by the lonely mountains, in this beautiful valley, where the smoke curls over the American jackal, emulating cities may spring up on this and the other side of the river; which together with the railroads will distribute, export, and handle the commerce of the world. If the El Paso Valley, ninety miles long and five miles wide, were growing in grapes, alfalfa, and onions we would be exporters at a fabulous profit. . . . "

Blacker commented that the Governor of Texas said that if he were a young man "he would settle in the valley of El Paso, with the firm belief that it would be within his power to become a millionaire—that it was the best and last place in the United States to make a fortune in a single lifetime."[4]

As Blacker finished talking, it was announced that the next speech would be given at Schutz Hall. In the meantime, everyone was invited to inspect the train.

It had been a hectic week for those now milling about the steam engine, climbing on the firebox, and passing through the fireman's cab. Nearly everyone within a forty mile radius showed up in town. Ever since the railroad announced intentions of building to the Pass of the North, new residents had been drifting in from every portion of the United States and Canada. Within the last few months the population had jumped from less than 800 to nearly 1500 souls.

Many people journeyed from across the Rio Grande at Paso del Norte. Don Espiridon Provencio, present as a representive of the Mexican people, was scheduled to speak later. Also, just plain Juan Q. Citizen had been traversing the Rio Grande all morning on the jerry-built ferry. Swarms of people traveled from as far away as Ysleta, Socorro, and even San Elizario, twenty-five miles down-river.

A mile or so west of El Paso, Fort Bliss disgorged its troops, particularly the officers, to join the celebration. These soldiers had spent hours decorating Schutz Hall with foliage and flowers. Now the room looked ready for the second round of speech making, the front seats "conspicious by the most beautiful of ladies and their families."

When the honored railroad guests had taken their places, Judge James P. Hague stepped forward to deliver the major address of the day. "California and Texas have struck hands," he said. "The railroad is the establishment of power; a controlling factor of that power is commerce; and the relations of commerce are ever those of friendship."

"The coming of the railroad," continued Mr. Hague, "has today spread before us . . . and enlivened our business; it has gladdened our hearts and given our homes a cheer, for even the little ones are eager to know its meaning."[5]

After the banquet, a full five hundred ladies and gentlemen gathered at the Central Hotel and danced to the tunes of a group of musicians from Paso del Norte. The Mexican aggregation did their best to play passable variations of waltzes, schottishes, gallops, polkas, quadrilles, and Virginia reels. As the evening wore on and the liquor flowed it did not matter to a single one of the five hundred ladies and gentlemen that a Mexican accent pervaded the music here and there.

Dallas Stoudenmire laughed, joked, and drank with the participants. His sister Virginia came by once with her husband Stanley M. "Doc" Cummings; and brother Dallas commented favorably on her black cashmere dress and coral jewelry. Then he moved on among the merrymakers, his light reddish hair glistening in the lamplight. One lady stopped him. She looked small beside his six-foot, two-inch frame. "I always thought your eyes were blue," she said.

"No, Ma'am! They're hazel!"[6]

A reporter for the El Paso *Herald* caught Stoudenmire's arm and briefly asked what he thought of the hilarity.

The marshal had a quip as fast as his trigger finger. "I'd like to see a railroad celebration and ball every day of the year."

The reporter mentioned that the next gala event was scheduled for the arrival of the Atchison, Topeka, and Santa Fe Railroad on June 11.

Marshal Stoudenmire beamed as if contemplating another "seventeen gallons of wine, a dozen bottles of champagne, and three and one half gallons of other bottled refreshments." Then he hoisted his drink, swirled it around in an amber colored, barrel-shaped glass, rubbed his granite chin, winked at the reporter, and sauntered on. Occasionally he paused to shake hands, give a pat on the back, or accept another drink—something he never turned down.

The *Herald* took particular note of the James Gilletts. The sergeant appeared with his wife, the former Helen Baylor. She was the sixteen-year-old daughter of her husband's commanding officer. Helen attended in her wedding dress and was voted by the ladies as "the most graceful dancer in the room."[7]

Oddly enough, the newspaper failed to mention any of the personalities who were to become such bitter enemies of Dallas Stoudenmire in the days to come. None of the Manning brothers was present, nor were W. W. Mills and Captain Baylor. Although the marshal had already collided with the Mannings, his troubles with Mills and the ranger captain had not yet materialized.

As the darkness grew deeper, the participants at the ball gradually wore themselves out. About eleven o'clock, the railroad executives excused themselves and started their journey back to California. El Pasoans went to bed, Paso del Norte residents re-crossed the river, and visitors from outlying ranches and communities stayed over until Friday. It had been a long and exciting day.

Ed Scotten, James Gillett's assistant marshal. Courtesy University of Texas at El Paso.

William Hale, John Hale's only son. Courtesy Reyes Madina.

Wife and children of Johnny Hale. Courtesy Mrs. Ester Maldonado.

Dallas Stoudenmire and two unidentified gentlemen in 1881. Courtesy Division of Manuscripts, University of Oklahoma Library.

Sgt. J. B. Gillett (right), Texas ranger and marshal of El Paso, and L. S. Turnbo, Texas ranger and first sheriff of Pecos, Texas. Courtesy Division of Manuscripts, University of Oklahoma Library.

Captain George W. Baylor, Texas ranger. Courtesy Division of
Manuscripts, University of Oklahoma Library.

Interior of the Gem Saloon. Courtesy the Aultman Collection,
El Paso Public Library.

Dallas Stoudenmire as marshal of El Paso. Courtesy the Aultman Collection, El Paso Public Library.

Dallas Stoudenmire's pocket gun. Courtesy Gordon Frost.

El Paso street, scene of shootout between Stoudenmire and John Hale, George Campbell, and Gus Krempkau. This is also where Stoudenmire was later killed. From the author's collection.

W. W. Mills, staunch Stoudenmire enemy. Courtesy of University of Texas at El Paso.

Joseph Magoffin, alderman and mayor of El Paso. Courtesy University of Texas at El Paso.

George Felix "Doc" Manning (right) with his son in 1917. Doc's arm which he holds behind his back was crippled by Dallas Stoudenmire's bullet. Courtesy Mrs. Lois Manning.

James Manning. Courtesy Frank Manning, El Paso.

George Felix "Doc" Manning family. Photograph probably taken in Flagstaff, Arizona, about 1890. Left to right: Tom, George Felix, Frank, Julia, and wife Sarah E. Alexander Manning. Courtesy Mrs. Adamarie Jones Manning Pastrana.

James Manning (seated); Frank Manning (brother of James, standing); Leonor Isabella Arozate Manning (wife of James); William Manning (son of James, seated on his father's lap). Photograph probably taken in El Paso around 1883–84. Courtesy Mrs. Adamarie Jones Manning Pastrana.

The Lone Star, El Paso's first modern newspaper, and a strong advocate of law and order. Courtesy University of Texas at El Paso Archives.

Photograph found on the body of Dallas Stoudenmire, probably either his sister Virginia (wife of Doc Cummings), or his wife Belle. Courtesy Gordon Frost.

chapter 7 CRIME BUSTING—EL PASO STYLE

DALLAS STOUDENMIRE was much more than a mere hired killer for the city of El Paso. He worked the city jail prisoners, kept the streets in good repair, enforced nearly all the various legal ordinances, collected fines and sometimes taxes, and policed the opium dens throughout the city, of which there were over a half dozen.[1] All of the odd and unusual chores fell to him also, the *Lone Star* of October 19 reporting that he "decreased the number of worthless curs." Since a city law required that a dog owner pay a two-dollar yearly tax, many animals ran loose and it became the marshal's duty to shoot them.

Heretofore, Stoudenmire's abilities as a sleuth have been little noticed. Yet, had he not killed anyone, his reputation as a detective should have ranked him high as an early day lawman. He applied common sense to the chore and was personally honest. No corruption or bribery has ever been attached to his name. In frontier El Paso this stood as an unbelievable record.

The city took pride in its marshal (at least in the beginning), and this esteem was more than repaid by him. Stoudenmire became not only the first marshal to take his work seriously, but the first to insist that his men wear identifiable dress. So far as he was concerned, the days of assistant marshals lolling about town with nothing more to indicate who they were than fast guns on their hips was over. He personally obtained enough money to purchase and present to his deputies handsome badges for their hats, the emblem shaped in the form of a gold leaf which encircled the words "Assistant Marshal—El Paso."[2]

Marshal Stoudenmire himself sported a solid gold badge, a token of affection from a friend named J. Johnson in Fort Worth.[3] This star, along with a brace of silver-mounted, Colt '71-'72, open top, .44 caliber, six-shot, single action revolvers (also a gift from a friend), became the working part of his trademark in El Paso.

Heretofore it has been generally accepted that Marshal Stoudenmire carried both pistols in leather-lined pockets. Although no solid evidence has been forthcoming to back these remarks up, conjecture of a more positive nature is now available and more reasonable conclusions can be drawn. Stoudenmire's Colts are originally thought to have had seven-and-one-half inch barrels, but at least one of these has had the barrel sawed off and is now in the possession of Gordon Frost, world-renowned El Paso gun collector. Frost decribes this revolver as having a sawed-off two-and-seven-eights inch barrel, with front sights and cartridge ejector missing. "It is the most deadly and efficient looking weapon I have ever encountered," Frost said.[4]

Probably Stoudenmire carried the sawed-off pistol in a form-fitting, leather-lined front pocket—his left—since Dallas is believed to have been left handed.[5] This was not an unusual practice; many gunmen did it in the old West. Technically, this pocket gun remained out of sight, allowing the carrier to visit church and attend to his normal business while being fully armed. Professionals like Dallas Stoudenmire, however, went a little beyond the common usage. Front sights and cartridge ejectors were apt to snag during the fast draw; consequently these items, together with a long barrel, were the first things to go.

Designed for short-range, arm's-length combat, the gun had no need for a sight. Called a "bellygun," it was more often that not rammed into an opponent's stomach and the trigger pulled. There was no need for a fast ejection system either, because after using this gun you were either alive or dead and reloading matters were not generally of serious importance.

Because of its extreme inaccuracy at ordinary shooting distances (even as far as across the street), this type of gun was usually of secondary significance. Reliance always fell on the more accurate, longer-barreled revolver, a kind nearly impossible to carry in the trousers because it was apt to snag, was to slow to whip into action, and had serious falling-out problems. In addition, the long-barreled guns were bulky and awkward while stuck inside the clothing and made it uncomfortable to sit down.

A conclusion seems inescapable, therefore, that in addition to a "pocket gun," Dallas probably carried an ordinary size .44 Colt, butt forward in the right hand hip holster, and made a cross draw. This system made both weapons convenient to the left hand without being bulky or awkward, and thus Stoudenmire could easily use whichever one suited his purposes.

Although the marshal took pride in his assistants, his men, unfortunately, did not always measure up to his trust or his expectations. Deputies generally came from the dregs of the community. Pay was poor and the hazards were great. Consequently, while many were able men and usually performed well, considering the circumstances, they were still a rough, coarse, and violent lot. They had to be in order to survive.

Deputies came and went so regularly (officially they could be discharged only by the city council), that the average citizen and even the aldermen had trouble knowing from week to week who was and was not a member of El Paso's infant police force.

An example of some of this confusion is found in the official minutes of the city council. Notations take cognizance of the fact that good deputies were difficult to find.

On April 15, 1881, A. S. and J. W. Jones signed on as deputy marshals. Both men were former Texas Rangers lured away from the force by the promise of seventy-five dollars a month that El Paso paid its deputies. On May 7, Frank Dawson signed as a Stoudenmire man. On June 1, both Jones boys resigned and were replaced by former Texas Rangers M. B. DeJanutt and J. W. Rodgers.

Then Dawson and Rodgers resigned on June 26 followed by DeJanutt on July 29.

On December 24, 1881, Assistant Marshal H. M. Mathis (believed to have been "Mysterious Dave" Mather),[6] obviously carrying the blessings of Dallas Stoudenmire, went before the city council and requested a salary increase from $75 to $125 a month. Mathis read and explained a letter which he had written himself, asserting that he had been the night officer for five months. His petition stated that the present wages were "barely sufficient to meet room and board."

After considerable haggling, the councilmen could not agree on what to do. A vote for a raise resulted in a three-to-three tie. Joseph Magoffin, who had only recently taken office as mayor, faced the unhappy duty of breaking a deadlock. He wavered and finally refused to go along with the pay increase.

Mathis then angrily jerked another letter from his pocket, this missive dated December 18: "I tender my resignation . . . as the pay is not sufficient for the work done and the risk assumed."[7]

Now and then an assistant marshal left office in a furor of publicity—all of it bad. William M. Page was one of these; and a tougher, more hard-nosed gunman never wore one of Stoudenmire's deputy emblems. Page's downfall occurred when an Arab visitor sought to purchase photographs from a merchant named Sprinz. A language barrier blocked most of the bargaining and discussions finally slacked off. Accustomed as he had been to bargaining techniques, Sprinz slyly gave the impression that his final offer had been made. He threw up his hands, shoved the pictures back in the drawer, and pretended he was leaving—obviously hoping that the Arab would hurriedly meet his price.

The Arab had already paid out several dollars in Mexican money, however, and assumed that he was now about to lose both the money and the photos. He ran behind the counter, jerked the drawer open and attempted to recover his *pesos* by helping himself to the merchant's till. Sprinz started screaming and summoned Page to arrest the culprit.

Page came on the run and soon had the highly indignant Arab marching toward the jail. This proved to be a slow procedure since the visitor repeatedly protested his innocence and kept pausing to argue his case. These tactics infuriated Page and he tired of dragging his prisoner along. With a crashing blow of his pistol, he sent the Arab sprawling into the street. Then changing his mind about jailing the man, the deputy hauled him before Mayor Magoffin who served as a judge. Magoffin assessed a fine of one dollar and court costs.[8]

Now it became the officer's turn to appear in court. Justice of the Peace Johnson accused Page of unwarrantedly striking and maltreating a prisoner. Page was bound over by the Grand Jury, which indicted him for "aggravated assault upon a man, a peddler commonly known as Arab, the name of whom it is to the Grand Jury unknown, and a further description of the person injured the Grand Jury is unable to find out."[9]

When trial time arrived, the judge noted that the Arab was no longer in the community, so charges against Assistant Marshal Page were dropped.[10]

The city council now requested Page's resignation. He complied bitterly and scratched out a note complaining that he had "always endeavored to discharge my duties as an officer, but . . . having been censured for my action in making an arrest last week, I wish to no longer remain in this position."[11]

There were councilmen who sympathized with Page. Had it not been for the uproar created by the press, the aldermen would probably never have asked for his resignation. Then, as now, the printed word swung a sharp sword in El Paso politics. Nevertheless, Alderman James P. Hague summoned enough courage to introduce a resolution thanking Page for his services.

Of course, all of Stoudenmire's assistants were not outstanding failures. Some of them turned out to be excellent choices.

James B. Gillett was recognized by any standards as the most outstanding assistant that Stoudenmire ever acquired. On December 10, 1881, Gillett replaced Deputy Mathis, who resigned in a huff over the money dispute. It was Dallas Stoudenmire who talked Gillett into leaving the rangers and working for the city. Earlier the two men had discussed this as they jointly delivered Joe E. Bright to the authorities at Deming, New Mexico. Bright had been living under the shadow of an indictment charging him with stealing $2,000 of his partner's money. Marshal Stoudenmire received a $500 reward for the capture.[12]

Officially speaking, when James Gillett received his appointment, his boss, Dallas Stoudenmire, was on the skids and rapidly approaching outright discharge. The marshal's heavy drinking was rapidly becoming both a tragedy to himself and to the city of El Paso. Already the council was taking another look at his qualifications for marshal. One wonders if Stoudenmire ever thought of Gillett as his possible replacement. Even if so, the marshal remained friendly with his assistant and exhibited no signs of jealousy.

El Paso always had enough firepower in the hands of Stoudenmire and company to manage any emergency. Yet, even with the most efficient police department, to incarcerate a prisoner in the shack which served as a jail seemed a folly of the highest order. Once in a fit of despair, the *Lone Star* editorialized that any felon seeking freedom could cut his way out of prison with a jackknife in two hours.[13]

Therefore the city ordered two iron cages from a firm in Chicago at the cost of $900 each. Blueprints sent to the company denote that El Paso showed no interest in coddling its prisoners. The "cages," as the newspapers came to call them, were not too far removed from the medieval iron maiden. Only spikes were missing from the inside.

Not aesthetically designed, the cages were eight feet long, seven feet wide, and seven feet high. Solid one-fourth-inch sheet iron spread over the top, bottom, sides, and rear. Only the front door had a barred area. Holes were perforated in the top to "allow foul air to escape," a wise precaution considering the 90-degree summer heat and the paucity of soap and water. Inside squatted two skimpy canvas bunks—"made of the best materials." A room to house these two cells was rented from John Dougher for $15 a month.[14]

Prisoners soon began arriving. One of the first to sample El Paso hospitality was Chris Moesner, regarded as a dangerous man in the mining community of Lake Valley, New Mexico. A Lake Valley gunman named Hood had kicked him around and threatened to "shoot his damn liver out."

When trouble first erupted, Chris Moesner and Dr.

Alex Kallenberg were visiting in the home of a friend, Dave Lufkin. As they chatted, Hood approached the house and challenged Moesner to come out and fight. Dave Lufkin, however, took Moesner's side. He disarmed Hood and threw him off the property.

Late that afternoon, Moesner noticed Hood returning with a rifle. Chris slipped quietly out of the house, intending to circle the bully and kill him. The plan worked well until Moesner opened fire. Unfortunately he completely missed his intended target and accidently sent a ball through the shoulder of Dave Lufkin and into the heart of Dr. Kallenberg, killing the doctor instantly.[15]

Chris Moesner did not wait around to offer assistance or to answer for the consequences of his poor shooting. As reward posters went up all over the Southwest offering $500 for his body dead or alive, he fled to Paso del Note, Mexico.

Marshal Stoudenmire soon discovered that Chris Moesner lived across the river. On December 13, 1881, Dallas and the Mexican authorities arrested him. Within a week Stoudenmire had delivered the fugitive to the Lake Valley authorities and happily returned to El Paso with the $500 tucked in his pocket.[16]

During the December of Moesner's arrest, Ben Schuster lodged a complaint with Marshal Stoudenmire, saying that his store had been burglarized and four Winchester rifles and several revolvers were missing.

Upon inspecting Schuster's place of business, Stoudenmire rightly noted that force had not been used to gain entrance. Correct reasoning told him that the thefts had been committed by an employee. Working with a list of names submitted to him, Dallas gradually narrowed the suspects down to one Eulalio Provencio, a young Mexican boy who handled odd jobs at the store.

After dark Stoudenmire, Gillett, and Schuster swooped down on Provencio's residence and placed him under arrest. A search of the home failed to turn up any of the stolen items.

Still satisfied that he had the right man, Dallas continued his questioning at the marshal's office. After several hours of intensive interrogation, however, the boy had not confessed and the marshal seemed no closer to a solution. The only alternative lay in frightening the suspect. Provencio was pulled to his feet. Stoudenmire removed his pistol, spun the cylinder a few times for sound effects, and took care to hold the black hole of the barrel directly under the boy's nose. Motioning to Gillett, Stoudenmire remarked that it was time for everyone to go for a walk. The prisoner marched in front to the outskirts of town, everyone pacing to the very audible cadence of Marshal Stoudenmire cocking and uncocking his revolver.

They were plodding into the sandhills when Provencio suddenly lost his composure, dropped to his knees, and began to babble the whole story. He implicated not only himself, but Jose Alarcon, another young Mexican. When picked up, Alarcon made a thorough confession, even admitting that they had stolen a bolt of cloth not previously missed.[17]

Stoudenmire's reputation began to spread beyond the boundary of El Paso. The Las Vegas (New Mexico) *Optic* commented on November 7, 1881, that "If every town had as good an item maker as officer Stoudenmire there would be fewer nuts to crack."

Apparently Stoudenmire spent considerable time helping New Mexico officials solve knotty crime problems. Ed Bartholomew, a specialist in Southwestern history, wrote a letter stating that he had notes on Dallas of about 1882 vintage when the marshal was in Lamy, New Mexico (near Santa Fe). Ed's note indicated that Stoudenmire worked with Deputy United States Marshal Tony Neis and together the two men gave the thugs at Lamy a going over. How many arrests were made is not known, but "Big Tony and Big Dal did not handle them with kid gloves."[18]

The *Optic* bears out some of Bartholomew's comments. On January 17, 1882, the newspaper noted that "Officer Stoudenmire of El Paso had a racket with a Lamy thug." This occurred at the railroad station in Lamy, the troublemakers being members of the old Hoodoo Brown gang from Las Vegas.[19]

Just a month prior to this date at the little railroad stop of Rincon, New Mexico, the call came for Stoudenmire to assist in preventing boxcar thefts. During a three-months' period, merchandise worth between twenty and forty thousand dollars had disappeared. The officials, hearing of Stoudenmire's ability at solving mysteries, sent for the young marshal and pleaded with him to catch the thieves. Methods employed were to be at his own discrestion. Dallas agreed to help and asked James H. White of the customhouse to assist. Both were deputized by the sheriff of Dona Ana County.

Things happened fast. On Wednesday, December 28, 1881, Stoudenmire and White arrived in Rincon. By midnight, Wombold, the railroad night watchman, and Hayden, a coal heaver, were in jail. On the following day Stoudenmire had a confession. Then as darkness fell, the fences, Mr. and Mrs. Procter, Dr. Paxton, and Charles Raitt, were also in confinement. Wombold and Hayden went on trial in Mesilla; the others were delivered to the Dona Ana County Sheriff at Las Cruces. The case was closed.[20]

All of these arrests carried the element of risk. Sometimes death laughed closer than anyone realized, for instance on November 5 when Stoudenmire and White passed through the El Paso railroad yards intent on making a routine arrest of a negro charged with assault. Unknown to the lawmen, there lurked another thug in one of the cars, a criminal more dangerous than the fellow sought. Wanted for murder, the gunman naturally assumed that the marshal carried a warrant for him and he braced himself to kill both officers if necessary. Fortunately, Stoudenmire and White, when nearly opposite the man, turned in another direction and the potential murderer, telling his story to a stranger at the depot, hurriedly boarded a fast-moving freight that was pulling out of the yards.[21]

Only a month later, on December 16, the marshal was again subject to an assassination attempt. A local rowdy named Joe King hid at the corner of Mrs. Marsh's boarding house, where Stoudenmire lived. At about three o'clock in the morning as Stoudenmire approached the residence, King opened fire from behind a pile of refuse. The assassin hid so near that the marshal was blinded by the gun flashes, although he pulled his own weapons and commenced firing in return. Both men woke up the town and burned a considerable amount of powder, all without success. King fled and a month later turned up in Harshaw, Arizona territory, bragging that he had shot the marshal and left town.[22]

chapter **8** STOUDENMIRE'S FEUD
WITH THE TEXAS RANGERS

$\mathbf{D}$URING THE civil war Reconstruction period,
Texas reverted to her old ways of lawlessness and Indian insurgency.
Outlaw rampages became so frequent that in 1874 the State commis-
sioned 450 rangers and from that day forward, the murderers, thieves,
robbers, highwaymen, redskins, smugglers, and so forth, were on their
way out of business. By 1879, wild Indians in particular were becoming
so hard to find that George W. Baylor enlisted in the ranger service and
specifically requested to be assigned to West Texas. He felt the
compulsion to kill Indians in roughly the same manner that some men
feel compelled to drink or gamble. Baylor thus acquired the honor of
participating in the last Indian fight in Texas. And while he was about
it, he brought a fear to lawbreakers that they had forgotten existed.

Captain George Baylor was a remarkable man with a
remarkable thirst for adventure. He was born at Fort Gibson, Indian
Territory, in 1832. An active secessionist, he enlisted in the Confederate army and served on Albert Sidney Johnston's staff, commanded a regiment in the Arizona Brigade, and saw service during the
Red River campaign of 1864. For his part in the battles of Mansfield

and Pleasant Hill, he was commended for gallantry. Unfortunately for him, these battles could not erase the stain on his record of April 6, 1864. At the Fannin Hotel in Houston, he and John Austin Wharton argued over "military matters." Wharton, unarmed, slapped Baylor's face and called him a liar. Baylor, furious, drew his pistol and killed Wharton.[1]

After the Civil War, Baylor secured a commission as a Texas Ranger, El Paso becoming a waystation in his travels and exploits. When peace and order had been restored to West Texas in 1882, the Captain's forces rode to Nolan County and assisted in putting down the "Fence Cutting War." Retirement from the rangers came in 1885 and death in San Antonio in 1916. Rumor had it that if he had liked to carve notches, a set of gunhandles could have been worn out.[2]

The Texas Rangers should not all be characterized as wandering Paladins. Most companies had more than their share of rottenness in the ranks. Understandably, this is a side of the rangers seldom mentioned. However, in fairness, the various ranger commanders acted diligently in thinning out the bad ones. Certainly a sorry reputation was never advertised as a prerequisite for gaining entrance. Nevertheless, this type of life and adventure attracted a hard type of man; and tucked away in obscure and generally unseen packets of the official ranger files are numerous names with the terse phrase "dishonorably discharged" scribbled alongside.

In many respects, the rangers just barely fell short of being outright bounty-hunters. Baylor's official correspondence makes numerous mentions of rangers who were more concerned about the size of a reward offered than in bringing a criminal to justice. Perhaps it was this lack of concern about the ordinary lawbreaker that prompted Major John B. Jones to send the following terse letter to Captain Baylor on November 27, 1880, six months before the advent of Dallas Stoudenmire:

> Citizens of El Paso County complain that your company does not use due diligence in hunting up and arresting white and Mexican fugitives from justice and sometimes think that you do not relish such work as this. They instance the case of Jesus Parda and several other noted thieves and fugitives from justice who live just across the river and make frequent visits to this side, and say they could be

caught if proper diligence was used. I do not know, of
course, whether these complaints are well founded, but
deem it proper to inform you of the fact that the complaint
is made and to remind you that it is the duty of all officers
and men in the frontier battalion to use all means in their
power to arrest all parties known or suspected to be
fugitives from justice or in any way violators of the law.
Unless you can make a good showing to the legislature of
work done by the frontier and special forces, you will not
likely get another appointment.

With all this in mind, it is easier to understand the
problems facing the ranger chiefs in West Texas. Baylor admitted he
had troubles, saying it was extremely difficult to find "some good men
who will take [an] interest in the service and have some State and
family pride to uphold."[3] Baylor also noted that there were no jails or
facilities for holding his prisoners, and he was too softhearted to chain
them to a tree and let them broil in the sun.

Men for ranger service were rarely transferred from
other regions. It was cheaper and easier to recruit them from nearby
locations, the companies generally stocking their ranks with local farm
and ranch boys. Around El Paso, however, the pickings were less than
choice. Those who enlisted were often running from the law. Ranger
service gave them something to do while they were between jobs in the
outlaw business.

Lieutenant John Tays told George Baylor that after
his ranger command broke up following the Salt War, nine ex-rangers
were killed as highwaymen in less than two years.[4]

Unfit and unqualified rangers plagued Baylor. He
cited the case of Ranger Herman Chipman of San Antonio, a lad who
the captain admitted was not too bright. Ranger Chipman had induced
Henry Southerland to assist in stealing five horses from a Mexican who
lived below Socorro, a few miles below the Ysleta rangers camp. Bad
luck immediately set in. The owner (known only as Abeytia) and his
two brothers overhauled the rustlers and killed them both. Unfortunately, Abeytia died by gunfire along with the guide he had employed.[5]

It was only natural that friction sparks should be
fanned between El Paso City Marshal Dallas Stoudenmire and the
rangers. Each party lived rough and untamed—they hated regulations.

Law enforcement offered an opportunity to change the rules and participate in excitement without going to jail.

Friction developed, friction which should never have gotten out of hand. Why this came about is not known; certainly to begin with the rangers and Stoudenmire went together like adobe and straw. On the 23rd of April, 1881, even Baylor spoke a few kind words for Dallas in a letter to Captain Neal Coldwell: "The marshal they have here is an old Confederate soldier and was also in Co. A, Frontier Battalion [for] eleven months when General Jones first commanded. He has good grit and is a good shot. He is now [in trouble] with the boys in El Paso."

Originally the marshal thought well of the rangers and tried to cooperate with them. In a generous mood once, he approached their quarters in the Overland Building and remarked: "Boys, you are doing most of the work and getting nothing for it. I propose to do what is right. [Since] I get two dollars for every arrest, [for] every arrest you make I will give you a dollar."[6]

Something like this immediately appealed to the latent mercenary traits of the rangers, who admittedly were shamefully underpaid. Rubbing their hands, they all turned out in force at the very next soldier payday at Fort Bliss. Everyone smiled as the buffalo soldiers headed for the nearest saloons. Ranger Joe Waldie said to Frank Beaumont as they watched several blue coats stroll into Paul Keating's place. "Frank, that looks good to me. We will make a dollar or so before morning."

By dark, pandemonium had broken loose in the town and by midnight there was brawling in the streets. When the sun came up the next morning, thirty-two soldiers sprawled in jail, five or six tenderly holding broken heads.

Mayor Magoffin conducted the trials and as the judge slowly passed on the cases in front of him, a lieutenant entered the room. Walking up to the judge, he said, "I want my men."

"You can have them when I get through with them, young man," said Magoffin. "Take off your hat and have a seat."

This activity between the rangers and Stoudenmire marked a beginning of the end of good relations among the two groups. What happened is not clear. All of a sudden both factions developed an

intense dislike for each other and the situation never improved until the
day Stoudenmire resigned.

One of the first difficulties to occur happened when
Stoudenmire sent a complaint to John B. Jones, Captain Baylor's
superior. The contents of this letter are unknown; only Jones' reply is
available:[7]

> In reply to your letter of the 23rd [of May, 1881], I would
> say that Captain G. W. Baylor has heretofore been
> instructed to keep a guard at El Paso to assist the civil
> authorities and enforce the preservation of peace.
>
> As captain commanding a company of the Frontier
> Battalion, he is authorized to do as he pleases for the best
> interests of the State and Service and must use his own
> judgement of the matter of details or guards, as being on
> the spot, he can better judge of your necessities.

Nevertheless, in spite of the fact that Stoudenmire
and the rangers were having their differences, crime in the immediate
vicinity of El Paso took a sharp dip. The outlawry trade was simply not
prospering as of old. On September 27, 1881, General King wrote
Baylor that "I anticipate . . . the public service will require soon the
transfer of your company from its present station to Wheeler County in
the Panhandle, and establishment of a detatchment in Oldham County.

"Under these circumstances, I wish to know and
desire that you write me fully if yourself and company (or any part of
it and the number) desire to abide by the order of transfer. If none
want to transfer, the company will be mustered out and another
organized."

Baylor signified his willingness to comply with the
order, but he reckoned without taking into account the local residents.
Startled and alarmed, the El Paso citizens flashed a plea to General W.
H. King. Mayor Magoffin wrote the message and seventy of the leading
businessmen and politicians signed it—Stoudenmire and Doc Cummings
being notable exceptions.

> We the undersigned citizens of El Paso County, Texas,
> learning of the proposed removal of Captain Baylor and his
> Rangers from this county respectfully and urgently repre-
> sent:

That this section now more than ever imperatively needs the Rangers; that a band of hostile Indians are actually in this country, and Captain Baylor is ready to pursue them. But if he is withdrawn these Indians will soon learn the fact, and the settlers, imigrants and stockmen will be at the mercy of these savages.

Lawless characters and desperate adventurers from all parts of the county are moving in this direction. They hang upon the border of New Mexico, Mexico, and upon the sparsely settled border of Northwest Texas, and they would swarm in upon us just as soon as the fear of Captain Baylor and his men are removed. These characters . . . have been suppressed, driven out or kept at bay, and good order prevails.

We therefore most urgently urge that you will retain Captain Baylor and his men here until law and order have secured a more stronger footing. El Paso, Texas, October 6, 1881.

The petition did manage to keep the rangers near El Paso, but Dallas must have snickered as he read the letter. He knew much about the caliber of men stationed here. Some, like Sergeant Gillett, he respected. Others, such as Captain Baylor, he regarded as honest and perhaps capable, even though the marshal was rarely able to establish any satisfactory relationships with them.

Baylor, of course, seemed a contradictory person. Gillett described him as one who never smoked, drank, or told smutty stories; but described his charges against entrenched Indian positions as "suicidal." Gillett also noted, although not considering it a serious sin, that Baylor cared nothing for discipline and his entire command would sometimes be strung out for a mile or so during a march.[8]

Lieutenant C. L. Nevill once complained bitterly about Baylor. He told Major Jones that Baylor was too easygoing. "They impose on him and discipline is very lax."[9]

One of Baylor's worst faults was that he was too trusting. Outlaw confederates were repeatedly able to work themselves into the ranger force and Captain Baylor would admit it. "It is the constant aim of the rustlers to get a spy into my camp and I feel quite sure that they have several times been successful."[10]

This candid remark seems an awesome understatement of the actual facts. In reality, he occasionally commanded as many spies as he did rangers. Weldon, Peveler, and Johnson (not the ex-marshal) figured in the situation which led up to the killing of Krempkau, Hale, and Campbell. George Campbell may have been an ex-ranger. Ranger Chipman was killed while rustling livestock. Private Bond journeyed to the graveyard after shooting up the town of Deming, New Mexico. Privates Bassett and Scotten admitted friendship with the rustling gangs and were discharged. The situation became so bad that the outlaw brigades knew more about ranger movements than the honest citizens did.

As Stoudenmire's dislike for the rangers grew more intense, he found it particularly galling to see them associate with the Manning brothers, his hated enemies. When up from Ysleta, the state officers spent their spare time mostly in either Jim Manning's Coliseum Variety Theater or Frank Manning's saloon. Two of Jim Manning's favorite rangers were Ed Scotten and Frank Scott, no relation. These two were supplied with everything—and everything included plenty of money, whiskey, and girls. So many girls were in evidence that the other rangers grew embarrassed and referred to their errant comrades as "whore pimps." Some rangers even openly suggested to Baylor that the two men be discharged, but Baylor, softhearted and shorthanded, appeared reluctant to let them go.

Baylor perhaps made a mistake in not listening to the judgment of his men, for Scott and Scotten ignited the final explosion which permanently prevented any opportunity for good relations between Stoudenmire and the rangers.

Difficulties began with hard liquor. While drinking, Frank Scott uttered some unflattering remarks about Marshal Stoudenmire, remarks which were not recorded for posterity. Soon the gist of the insults blew along the street to the marshal's office. Dallas heard about it, spoke to Gillett, and together they headed for the Coliseum Theater. Moments later, Stoudenmire had slammed through the saloon doors, backed Scott into a corner and called him to account. According to witnesses, superlatives about Scott were used which caused even calloused saloon customers to blanch.[11]

Baylor said Stoudenmire referred to Scott as a "thirty-dollar-a-month son of a bitch, said none of them [rangers] would fight, that he could whip them all, clean up the Mannings, and was king of the world."[12] If Baylor was not exaggerating some of Stoudenmire's statements, the remarks were certainly an indication of the marshal's alcoholic state of mind.

It just so happened that four other rangers were drinking in the same room with Scott, although not in his company. Only two are identifiable, those being Kirk Turbo and J. M. Deaver. Turbo shuffled his feet in embarrassment, not sure if he should be angry at Stoudenmire or Scott. Deaver, a part-time stage driver, merely leaned against the wall and looked on.

Suddenly Deaver had a premonition that he should move, and as he did so he noticed a small, round, black opening behind him. Gillett noticed it too, plus some similar holes in the adobe walls. Nudging Stoudenmire, he said, "Lets get out of here."

Dallas did not want to leave. His cussing stride was just stretching out to a pace befitting the subject. Yet he was not a fool. He took in the situation and followed Gillett into the street.

As the lawmen left, Jim Manning walked into the room, and a relieved Scott introduced him to his ranger friends.

"My God, man," Jim yelled. "Why did you not tell me these were your friends. Come back here and let me show you something."

Trooping single file into the adjoining room, the rangers witnessed the reason for Jim Manning's alarm. They had nearly become battle casualties. Along the wall stretched three cots with shotguns on top. Three holes were bored in the wall, the openings just large enough to allow a shotgun to poke through. One or more gunmen stationed here could cover every square inch of the barroom. Jim Manning and others had been closely watching the argument. Had the situation gone much further, Manning and his men would have saturated the room with flying buckshot.

Dallas Stoudenmire snorted with anger and frustration as he walked back to his office, more upset at the rangers than at the Manning brothers. That afternoon, March 29, 1882, he drafted the following dispatch to General King:

> When I assumed the duties of City Marshal of this town, I encountered difficulties unpleasant as well as unwholesome to myself. In the discharge of these duties—the object of

which was the preservation of peace and the enforcement of the laws—I called on all offenders and law abiding citizens to assist.

Among the former were a lot of rangers stationed in this portion of the State who have ran most ingloriously when called to the scratch.[13] I have found them ever since most untrustworthy and unreliable. I can even go further and say I have always found them more ready to aggravate than to preserve the public peace; as well as taking sides with the lawless rather than the law abiding portion of the town.

They—for some reason or the other unknown to me—take great delight in throwing obstructions in my way whilst in the discharge of my duties. They come to town fully armed and remain as long as they please, get full and go back to camp shooting through the streets. I have been able to manage the criminal element of this place thus far without their assistance—and much easier had they been absent—and think that I can continue to do so in the future. I have spoken to Col. Baylor—a gentleman for whom I have the highest respect—on several occasions to keep them in camp, but without any success. The town is not in the state of quiet that I would like, and am satisfied that if any trouble should come up I would have more serious trouble if they were here than I would if they were absent. These, General, are the facts in the case, and I ask you as a personal favor that they be kept out of this place and at their proper duties. If they are bound to loiter about town, I ask only that they be compelled to keep their arms in camp. I not only ask this in my own behalf, but also in behalf of the law abiding portion of this city.

Hoping you will give this your immediate attention, I remain, yours respectfully,

Dallas Stoudenmire
City Marshal
El Paso, Texas

Upon receipt of Stoudenmire's message, General King asked Captain Baylor for an explanation. Defending himself, the captain wrote a long rambling essay in which he reviewed most of the incidents taking place within the last year or so.

"I was greatly astonished at the tenor of his letter,"

Baylor wrote. "I can assure you that either he used the long bow in his attack on the rangers or my memory is sadly at fault. I take it for granted that he was either drunk or under the influence of opium."[14]

Nevertheless, Baylor did move his company back to Ysleta on April 24.

In all other respects, the ranger status in town remained about the same. At the ranger camp, however, heavy arguments were raging. Several rangers were considerably irked at Marshal Stoudenmire's references to them as "thirty-dollar a month sons of bitches who would not fight." Defending Stoudenmire were some of the older rangers; it was their opinion that the rangers had allowed themselves to be led into the mess by the actions of Scott and Scotten.

A red-headed youth named C. L. Hathaway felt that Stoudenmire was entirely in the wrong and an apology should be forthcoming. Hathaway was a harmless-looking individual who tried to make up for his passive appearance by habitually wearing two long forty-fives strapped on his hip. The other rangers had a tendency to snicker when the red-headed boy was around, but the snide remarks deterred Hathaway not at all. He always took the kidding in stride, giving back as much as he received.

In particular, Hathaway was concerned over the charge of cowardice leveled at his company. Early one morning he buckled on his long-barreled guns and rode to town. Dismounting and meeting Dallas on the street, he snapped, "I understand that you made the remark that no thirty-dollar-a-month son of a bitch would fight."

Taken back momentarily, Dallas wasn't sure whether to grin or spank the impudent youngster.

Continuing, Hathaway said, "I am a private in the ranks of the Texas Rangers, but I am not a son of a bitch."

Stoudenmire felt the humor in the situation and what's more, he was beginning to like Private Hathaway. Putting on his straightest and most sober face, he apologized. "The Texas Rangers as a body of men are gentlemen, but skunks can get into the service," Dallas said.

When the conversation was finished, Hathaway was satisfied. Highly elated, he galloped back to Ysleta and became the hero of the camp.[15]

When the trouble between Marshal Stoudenmire and the rangers first broke out, his deputies (many of them former rangers), tried to convince Dallas that he was wrong. These pleas generally had little effect; Stoudenmire was drinking heavily and showed little inclination to admit any of his faults.

Frank Beaumont, an ex-ranger currently working for E. Germain and Company, in particular had aroused the marshal's ire, all for reasons which Beaumont did not know or would not state.

One morning toward the close of Stoudenmire's term as marshal, Beaumont met deputy Nep DeJanutt, jolly drunk, walking down El Paso Street. "Frank, there is Stoudenmire on the corner," DeJanutt said. "Come with me. He must shake hands with you and make up; he is entirely in the wrong."

"Not this morning," Frank replied. "The marshal is without doubt drunk and where will I stand."

"You come along," the insistant Nep said. "I will see that he does nothing rash."

Beaumont allowed himself to be taken by the arm and led up the street where Stoudenmire was found stone sober. "Dallas," DeJanutt said, "shake hands with Frank. He has never done you any wrong."

Dallas, with a half friendly grin on his face, glanced over at Beaumont. "I have no objection; shake Frank."

Although Stoudenmire was sober and able to reason rationally on this occasion, his mood, with the consumpion of liquor, changed shortly thereafter.

Frank Beaumont had changed jobs and was on his way to work at the *Lone Star* when he stopped to speak with Ranger Ed Scotten in the street.

A few moments later an intoxicated Stoudenmire approached, busily rolling up the sleeves of his linen duster. "How are you, Scotten?" Dallas asked. "I came near killing a scoundrel just now. I wish I had."

Beaumont knew that this was no place for him, so he hastily said his goodbys and started to leave.

"Stop right there, Beaumont. I want to tell you what I think of you," Stoudenmire snarled.

For what seemed an eternity Stoudenmire cussed Beaumont, finally turning and striding into the Alamo saloon.

Beaumont, so angry he was wiping tears away, stopped at Frank Manning's saloon and told Frank his troubles. Manning immediately saw a method for getting rid of Stoudenmire. Passing a shotgun across the bar, he grunted, "This is as good a time as any to settle this thing. Go down and shoot the devil out of him."

Together Manning and Beaumont walked down to the Alamo and Manning stepped off to the side where he could watch a man die. Beaumont stood there in front of the saloon, cocking and uncocking the shotgun. Although he waited and waited, Stoudenmire never strode through the door. Around dark, Beaumont, much calmer now and thinking more rationally, went home.

He learned later that Stoudenmire, upon entering the saloon, bellied up to the bar and proceeded to drink himself unconscious, finally falling to the floor where in a drunken slumber he spent the rest of the afternoon and part of the evening.[16]

chapter **9** THE STRANGE LIFE & DEATH OF
STANLEY M. "DOC" CUMMINGS

NEAR MACON County, Alabama, where Dallas Stoudenmire grew up, and in North and South Carolina from whence the Stoudenmire clan seems to have migrated, the name Cummings is a familiar one. Perhaps Dallas and Doc knew each other previously. Perhaps not. Existing records are incomplete.

The two men at least became acquainted in Texas during the early 1870s. On December 10, 1874, at about the time Dallas Stoudenmire was taking his discharge from the Texas Rangers, Stanley M. Cummings married Virginia Stoudenmire May at Columbus, Texas.[1] Her former husband, Mr. I. C. B. May, had apparently died—at least there is no record of any divorce.

From 1874 to 1879, Doc and Virginia drop out of sight. On Thursday, November 13, 1879, the Commissioners Court of Wheeler County (located in the Texas Panhandle) began debate on how properly to develop the unorganized counties attached to it. During this special session S. M. Cummings, an Oldham County resident, received an appointment as Justice of the Peace for Oldham, and thus the judicial growth of that county began. Shelton Edwards counted out the

LIFE AND DEATH OF "DOC" CUMMINGS

money for Cummings' official bond, the available records suggesting there is quite a tale behind that transaction, even if only a fraction of it is known.

Edwards, a shrewd confidence man from New York, came to the Panhandle and entered into a business partnership with two Jewish brothers, John and Will Cone, who had formerly lived in Big Spring and Tascosa, Texas. In 1879, they migrated from Tascosa and with Edwards formed a company in Oldham County. First fruits of this association was a criminal charge leveled against all three of the partners, an accusation that they had sold "manufactured goods, cigars, tobacco, and liquor at retail without paying the special tax."[2]

Early in 1880 the firm of Edwards and Cone fell into more trouble. Edwards had forged some papers and persuaded an old, senile rancher to part with his sheep. The animals were subsequently sold and the swindler purchased six wagons and eighteen oxen with the money. However, the old man had his occasional moments of clear thinking and during one of these periods he began fussing with Edwards for the return of everything that had been taken. Immediately, Edwards tried to ease the fellow's mind by taking him to Las Vegas, New Mexico, where he promised the money would be returned. Installing the dupe in a hotel, Edwards vanished—never to be seen again.

The swindled man stormed angrily back to Texas, hired a lawyer, and preferred charges against the firm of Edwards and Cone. John Cone had to answer for his absent partner's transgressions; he heard judgment pronounced against the company for an unspecified sum.

Somehow Doc Cummings became involved in all this. Cone turned around and won a court suit against Doc for more than $1,400. Dockets do not reveal the reason for this legal action—but it must have been tied in with the civil suit John Cone lost due to the dishonest practices of his partner.

Cummings had no money. Consequently Cone took charge of 900 sheep to satisfy the judgment. All of this makes one wonder if these were the same sheep which Edwards illegally took from the old rancher.

Dallas Stoudenmire may have been mixed up in all this. He lived in the general vicinity at the time, his own account of

April 19, 1882, stating that he farmed and raised sheep with Cummings while Doc resided in the Panhandle.

On March 24, 1880, Commissioners Court noted that Doc Cummings' bondsman, Shelton Edwards, had left the state. Justice of the Peace Cummings was ordered to make a new bond. Although twenty days were allowed to qualify, Doc either could not or would not continue with the job. His resignation came on April 14, the replacement being James McMasters, who also failed to qualify within the prescribed time.[3]

Looking for something to do, Doc purchased on May 25, two acres of land from McMasters and others of the Houston East and West Texas Railroad Company. It is unknown what Cummings did with the property.

Apparently Doc was feeling restless and by October of 1880 he took his wife and small daughter to San Marcial, New Mexico. Here he entered the hotel business in what proved to be one of the roughest, most sinful railroad division points in the West. San Marcial is now only a vacant patch of desert; a raging flood washed the town away in 1929.

It was in San Marcial that Doc Cummings first built his fearsome reputation. James White, a prominent El Pasoan, knew Cummings there and described him as a dangerous man, "one who would carry into execution a threat which he had made against another."[4]

Doc was restless here also and decided to move to El Paso. During the stage trip he met George Washington Carrico, soon to become editor of the El Paso *Times*. Conversation between the two men was pleasant; Doc was on his good behavior and sober during the forty-mile ride between Mesilla, New Mexico, and El Paso. Carrico described Doc as an excellent traveling companion, "one who had every string leading from his heart to the grasp of his fellow man."[5]

Carrico did not speak as kindly of others. They arrived in El Paso on the night before Christmas Eve and there was no room at the inn. Doc Cummings, the editor, and another passenger named Dick Hardy spent their first night in town sleeping on the floor of the Central Hotel gambling room. Carrico raged that the hotel proprietor furnished only a copy of the *Police Gazette* for a blanket—and charged fifty cents for the accommodations.[6]

Doc Cummings opened several restaurants in El Paso, only one of which became sucessful. He installed one on San Antonio Street at a site later occupied by the Acme Saloon. Another opened in the Overland Building, one of the most prominent structures in El Paso. Neither were suitable for eating houses, however, and Doc closed them within a few days or weeks. Plans were then laid for a huge restaurant in Paso Del Norte,[7] but he never lived to see these expectations come into existence.

Doc's famous restaurant was the Globe on El Paso Street, two doors down from the corner of San Antonio. And what an elegant establishment it was! Advertised as the finest eating place west of Chicago and south of Denver, the tables were set with expensive silver and table cloths. Exotic food was imported from all over the world, which was how the Globe came by its name. Doors were open at all hours of the day or night. "We have only the best customers, ladies and gentlemen," one advertisement said. "No flies, dust, or noise," boasted another.

The business attracted so many paying customers that W. T. Hickok was hired to cater and manage.

This left Doc with too much time on his hands and although he liked the prestige of having the finest eating house in El Paso, he yearned for something with a little more action. On June 1, 1881, he enlisted as a private in the Texas Rangers and served under Captain Baylor at Ysleta. Discipline did not appeal to him, however; so on July 12, he asked for and received a discharge.[8]

Ex-Ranger Stoudenmire and ex-Ranger Cummings made an eye filling pair on the streets of El Paso. Dallas stood tall and lithe, standing probably an inch or so higher than his heavy-set brother-in-law. There is no available description of Doc Cummings; those people who described him made reference only to his "largeness."

Both Dallas Stoudenmire and Doc Cummings were exceptionally similar. They were heavy drinkers, were quick to fight, and possessed deep feelings of right and wrong—they were always right. Neither was above provoking a quarrel, or even killing a man if the end result seemed justified. They were slow to forgive. And both were intensely, even fiercely, loyal to each other.

As Stoudenmire took over law enforcement duties, Doc opened the Globe and received a contract to feed the city jail prisoners.[9] Doc also exhibited some sense of civic responsibility. He served as Second Ward presiding officer during the elections of August, 1881.[10]

In early February, 1882, a Kansas Sheriff rode through town on the trail of a rapist. Reportedly the criminal had ravished his victim back in the Sunflower state and fled south to Chihuahua, Mexico. Doc, an emotional chap, became enraged while listening to the sheriff and volunteered to assist in running the man down. A deputy's badge was pinned on Doc's shirt and he became a bonafide law officer, an important point to remember.

The two-man posse now crossed the Rio Grande and knifed deep into Mexico.[11]

They had hardly splashed across the boundary when Stoudenmire and Gillett both contracted an illness, the symptoms of which indicated influnenza. The marshal and his assistant were confined to bed.

Dallas recovered first, but he felt weak and unable to keep up with the demands of his job. A short vacation to Columbus, Texas, was prescribed as a cure. Perhaps he felt that getting married would help the cure along. In the office of Colorado County Judge Charles Riley, on February 20, he married Miss Isabella Sherrington.[12]

In the meantime, the Mexico posse had been un-successful and returned to El Paso. The sheriff journeyed back to Kansas. Gillett was still ill, so Doc decided he would keep his deputation, become the El Paso police force,[13] and clean out the "damn Mannings."

Doc's anger had been nursed along for months, ever since the preceding April when rumor had it that the Manning brothers had talked the drunken barfly Bill Johnson into an attempt on Stoudenmire's life. Jim Manning, in particular, was blamed by Doc as responsible for the ambush and Cummings told John Woods shortly after the bushwhacking incident that "we are going to string up all such men as he."[14]

Even months after the incident, Doc remained sen-sitive about the happening, and whenever he noticed Jim Manning on the street, an opportunity was never missed to mutter a threat. "That damn son of a bitch," Doc would say. "I only want a pretext to let his damn light out."[15]

Doc got his opportunity on February 14. As pieced together, the events went something like this:

About six o'clock, shortly after dark, Doc, who carried the customary snoot-full, walked into the Coliseum Variety Theater and found Jim Manning smoking a cigar. Jim was a reformed alcoholic who had been off the bottle for over a year. Doc knew this and used it as an excuse to provoke an argument; he ask Manning to take a drink.

"All right, I will. I'll have some cider," Jim said.

This irked Doc, but he decided to let it pass and needle Jim on another subject, so mention was made of a man named Gilson whom Cummings had seen down in Mexico. Apparently Gilson had been one of the gunmen who opened fire on both Doc and Dallas Stoudenmire the night ex-marshal Johnson attempted his assassination. The bushwhacker had left town when the vigilantes were organized and was afraid to come back.

"Doc, you are mistaken," Jim said.

"And you," Cummings snarled back, "are a God damn liar."

"Doc, what is the use of your using me this way? I thought that old thing had been settled some time ago."

Cummings then brought up the matter of a shotgun. He accused Jim of lending the gun to someone for the expressed purpose of killing Doc.

Manning denied the charge, claiming that no one had ever used the gun but himself.

Snapping back, Doc Called Jim another God damn liar and claimed that "We found the gun in a wagon where this party had left it.[16] I can't forget this. Are you fixed?"

The saloon owner replied that he was, but that he did not want trouble. Nevertheless, he removed his coat and hat, laying them on a soda water case near the bar. Stepping into the middle of the barroom, he cried, "Doc, what is the use of your forcing me to fight? Why can't we settle this in a peaceful manner?"

"Turn yourself loose; I am ready," Doc growled.

"Doc, let's settle this. I will get on my knees. I will do anything to settle it in a quiet way," Jim pleaded.

"You are a cowardly son of a bitch," Doc said. He then spoke of the other Manning brothers as being gentlemen, but continued to cuss Jim. He did, however, allow Manning to put back on his coat.

Now the conversation switched to the bartender. Doc kept growling that he stood ready to fight if the barkeep would keep his hands from under the counter.

"You don't have to talk to him," Jim said. "He has no gun behind the bar . . . besides, I do not hire bartenders to do my fighting."

"If I had a man work for me and he would not fight for me, I would kick his damn ass," Doc replied. "Let's go up the street."

Stepping outside a few paces and pausing in front of a furniture store, Doc grabbed Jim by the coat and decided he might as well get his slaying over with. "I think that I will kill you now."

At that moment a passerby, T. H. East, heard the commotion and strolled toward the sounds of voices. As he stepped close, Doc whirled and cracked, "You son of a bitch, what have you to do with this? Are you one of his friends?" A hard revolver barrel rammed East in the chest.

After an anxious second, East, who testified later at the inquest that he knew neither Cummings nor Manning, began to loudly squeal his innocence. After listening for a few minutes and spitting out a few more profanities, Doc allowed the man to journey on his way provided his hands remained in the air until the blackness of the night obscured him.

Smelling a killing in the air, East hurried to the Manning saloon where he found Frank and told him the story of how Jim was being corraled and about to be shot.[17]

When Doc turned to resume his quarrel, he found that his quarry had disappeared inside the Coliseum. So Cummings pushed his way through the doors and scowled as he walked to the bar. In a loud voice he told Jim Manning to take a drink. Jim once again refused and Doc took the refusal as a rejection of his company.

At this point the bartender, David Kling, interrupted the conversation, feeling that his two *pesos* of comment were needed. Doc turned his spleen on Kling and snarlingly told him to keep his hands above the counter. Protesting that he had no pistol hidden out of sight, Kling began to joke about the matter and offered to bet fifty dollars that no weapon lay concealed there.

Jim now walked behind the bar and ordered David Kling to leave as the fight was not his. Kling refused. He justified his presence by commenting that he had been hired to tend bar and he would not be frightened off. Saying nothing more, Jim walked past the north end of the bar and vanished inside the hallway where the ticket booth for the theatre stood.

Within a few minutes, he reappeared. His coat was off and his hand hung over a low slung pistol. Witnesses disagreed whether he stood near the bar when the shooting started, in the doorway, or a step or so back in the hall. Suddenly there he stood, ready to kill. "Doc, we will have this out," he snarled.

Cummings, who according to one witness appeared docile at the time and according to another had his right arm on the bar and in the act of taking a drink, spun into action a little late. Guns crashed from both sides of the saloon. Some men swore that Doc fired first; others were just as adamant in swearing it was Jim Manning.

To Doc it made little difference who had been the faster on the draw. His bullet sailed wild and smacked into the adobe wall, a little above and behind his opponent. Then feeling the shock of two heavy pistol balls in his body, he reeled across the room, crashed through the bat wing doors, collapsed, and died on El Paso Street. As he lay there in the road, he emitted one terrifying groan—then the street grew silent.

Officer William Page had been eating at the Globe when the guns cracked. He rushed to the scene, stepped over Doc's inert body, and found Jim Manning inside the saloon. Jim still grasped his weapon and Page turned it over to a Mr. Wade, police officer and jailer. Manning told Page in a dazed voice, "I have stood this thing as long as I could. I could not stand it any longer."

Page found Cummings' pistol in the hands of Frank

Manning, who had recently arrived. Frank claimed he had just removed it from Doc's limp hand. Examination of the revolver showed two empty chambers on oposite sides of the cylinder, this alone making Doc's gun the most unusual weapon in the West—a strange fact never looked into by the coroner's jury.

An examination of Jim Manning's pistol showed only one empty chamber, although Jim swore that he had fired both death bullets. His gun should be ranked as the second most unusual weapon.

After dawdling for days and scratching out sixty-three pages of testimony, the Coroner's jury reached a conclusion that S. M. Cummings had died from the effects of two bullets, one fired from the pistol of James Manning and the other from a person unknown. The whole town knew that bartender David Kling fired the second shot.

Jim Manning was charged with murder and placed in custody of the Texas Rangers. Bond was established at $1,000. Apparently he never went to trial; the newspapers are silent and there exist no court records concerning the case.

Although two bullets caused Doc's death, there were other suspicious aspects of the killing. After the shooting, Doc was removed and hauled a few doors away to Marcuses' Jewelry. His clothes were stripped off and the body examined by Drs. J. A. McKinney and King Ross. The physicians testified that either wound would have been fatal. Either bullet would have caused instant paralysis also; the point being that after absorbing the slugs, any shooting done by Cummings would have been mechanical and not something thought out. By the same token, the bullets did not strike Doc while he directly faced his man; instead Cummings was turned slightly away from his killer when the two bullets took effect—an indication that Cummings fired last.

The strangest and most stunning part of the physicians' testimony was yet to come. They swore that Doc also had a fractured skull, the break being on top of the head and a little toward the rear. Ross felt that the fracture probably came about when Cummings fell in the street. McKinney stated flatly that in his opinion the concussion could only have been caused by a pistol barrel smashing across the the top of the skull.[18]

When all the testimony has been balanced and

weighed, it seems evident that Doc brought about his own death. It was he who pushed the argument, although he may or may not have drawn first. His life was snuffed out not so much by Jim Manning as by his own hatreds, pugnacious temper, suspicions, and hard whiskey.

Interment was on February 18 in a small cemetery north of town by the Rio Grande Lodge, No. 23, Knights of Pythias.

Then all of El Paso settled back to await the return of the marshal, everyone wondering when the next round of bloodletting would begin.

chapter **10**   THE STOUDENMIRE–MANNING
BROTHERS FEUD

DALLAS STOUDENMIRE and Doc Cummings were more than friends and brothers-in-law; an exceptionally strong bond of admiration and trust held them together. As a team they had farmed, raised cattle and sheep, and probably gone into business. In El Paso, Doc advertised his Globe Restaurant as managed by Cummings and Company, Marshal Stoudenmire being the "Company."

On Saturday, February 25, 1882, Dallas Stoudenmire and his bride arrived in El Paso where James Gillett explained the details of the tragedy. The marshal's face blanched white while he listened. Overdue accounts to be settled with the Manning brothers were stacking up.

The feud between the two factions began to blaze after the start of Stoudenmire's administration. First Hale and Campbell had fallen before the marshal's smoking pistol. Then the Mannings sicked Bill Johnson on Stoudenmire, and Johnson toppled to his death carrying a volley of bullets in his chest. Now the brothers had evened everything by slaying Doc Cummings—and with Doc gone there were no others whom Dallas could depend upon. He stood all alone to face his enemies.

Of course, there was more to the Stoudenmire–Manning trouble than just the killings. A power struggle was involved. El Paso could support only one strong faction and the Mannings had arrived first. Naturally they resented any interlopers.

In particular, the brag reputedly made by Doc Cummings, "These fogies have run this town long enough; now we [supposedly himself and Dallas Stoudenmire] are going to run it to suit ourselves," did nothing to allay any feelings.

There is little in the Manning background to indicate a bent toward violence. The clan had been raised in well-to-do circumstances on a plantation near Huntsville, Alabama. In 1837, the eldest child, George Felix, was born. Several sisters followed, along with four brothers, Frank, James, John, and William. George Felix studied medicine at the University of Alabama until nearly thirty; then his father, Peyton Thomas Manning, sent him to Paris, France, to finish school. As the Civil War loomed, however, Felix received a call that his father was ill. So he dropped school and returned—just in time to meet his father's funeral procession moving along the road.[1]

In the fighting which followed, Felix became a lieutenant in the Confederate Army, serving honorably and well on General Joe Wheeler's staff.[2] James, John, and Frank were also soldiers. Frank's enlistment had a touch of pathos. Like brother William, Frank was too young to enlist, and for a while he did not mind. He had a girl; the two were very much in love, and the cannon shots seemed very far away. Suddenly she died or was killed. A brokenhearted Frank told his family that either they permit him to enlist or he would do so under an assumed name. With grieving hearts the Mannings relented and Frank donned the Confederate gray. For what it is worth, Frank cherished the girl's memory for the remainder of his life. He alone of the brothers never married.[3]

Like ordinary Southerners, the Mannings dedicated themselves to the cause of the Confederacy. Their patriotism went a little farther than the average, however. After Appomattox, they angrily resolved never to shave until the South had refought the war and won.[4] All four men kept their vow.

While waiting for the Dixie fortunes to revive, the brothers returned to Alabama, picked up William, and journeyed to

Texas. On the Gulf Coast they built a sloop, rigged it, outfitted it, and pointed it toward Mexico and South America. Details of how far they traveled are not available, but a family legend says they stopped somewhere in Mexico. Offering their fighting talents to Maximilian, the Mannings shot their way across that unhappy land until they were expelled after the Frenchman's execution.[5]

As mentioned, Dallas Stoudenmire may have spent a portion of his time in Mexico. Perhaps the two parties met under unfavorable circumstances, setting the precedent for the feud to be taken up with renewed fury in El Paso.

With Mexico off limits, the next resting place for the Manning brothers became Belton, Texas, where a sister Julia had recently married a man named Cummings.[6] This was not Doc Cummings; Julia's husband died of tuberculosis. He could have been a relative of Doc's however, maybe even a brother; and it is not beyond a possibility that friction developed here between Doc Cummings and the Mannings; and Dallas Stoudenmire was dragged into these troubles.

At the period of the Manning migration to Belton, the countryside writhed in the throes of a measles epidemic. A solitary doctor tussled with the problem and somehow talked George Felix into assisting. Felix had finished his medical training, but lacked a medical license since he had neglected to take the final examinations.[7] When the epidemic finally died out, the doctor convinced Felix that a medical diploma promised a key to his future. Manning agreed and in 1874 he graduated from the Medical College of Alabama.[8]

Dr. Manning opened his practice in Giddings, Lee County, Texas. The records show that he resided there from 1874 to 1878.[9] Here he became involved in a brutal knife fight, the first indication that his personality leaned toward the quarrelsome.

Dr. Manning and Dr. Molett became rival physicians and, as rivals often do, they argued bitterly. When the dispute could not be arbitrated peacefully, the two doctors agreed that the only gentlemanly way to settle the matter would be to kill each other. Off to the piney woods they went, bandages to dress their wounds dangling from their arms, and with no seconds or spectators, they drew their bowie knives and cautiously started to circle each other. Stripped to the waist, the combatants clashed, each taking a firm grip on the other's arm so that neither weapon could be used. By mutual consent they separated and warily watched for another opportunity to siphon blood.

After sparring for several minutes, they rushed together once more. Dr. Manning took a superficial cut on the neck while Dr. Molett received a more serious slice on the arm. Then the fighting paused while wounds were dressed.

With more respect for each other, the opponents feinted and dodged for another half hour. Molett finally caught Dr. Manning about the neck and twice stabbed him deeply in the chest. Manning retaliated by plunging his knife into Molett's back and giving it a wicked twist. The fight ended.

Dr. Manning collapsed and lay senseless. Molett staggered to his surgical tools and managed to bind his back. He meant to allow Dr. Manning to die. Still, the physician had a few humane instincts left and he returned to truss up Felix and save his life. Now both men had lost so much blood that they were unable to walk. Luckily some residents passed by and carried the antagonists into town where they spent weeks recovering.[10]

When his health improved, Dr. Manning returned to Belton where, in 1979, he married Miss Sarah E. Alexander.[11]

While Doc was practicing medicine and knife-fighting, James, Frank, John, and William were driving cattle between East Texas and Kansas, an occupation which carried more than its share of dangers. Somewhere, somehow, William was killed—bushwhacked and murdered according to the family. Relentless in vengeance, James, Frank, and John rode out in pursuit, overhauled the assassin, and shot him down. The Manning family believes to this day that Dallas Stoudenmire involved himself in the slaying.[12]

In any case, whatever the circumstances were, all of the brothers except Felix had drifted to El Paso by 1880. Dr. Manning had recently become a father and delayed going until nearly a year later. In 1881, he and his family took a stage, a hundred-mile trip to the railroad that would deliver them to West Texas. Burning ranches lay all along the route and the family worried about losing their hair to the scalping knife. An Indian marauding party swept across the land, fortunately terrorizing an area ahead of the Mannings and traveling in the same direction. On June 1, 1881, the Dr. Manning clan arrived in El Paso.[13]

Dr. Manning did not arrive early enough to witness any of Dallas Stoudenmire's handiwork with the pistol; but, as events developed, he actively supported his brothers in the dispute. Doc gained many friends, W. M. Coldwell referring to him not only as a reputable physician, but "probably the most accomplished gentlemen in early day El Paso."[14] City council minutes attest to the fact that he was one of the few doctors ministering to the impoverished sick.[15] Several times he became the only physician willing to treat smallpox patients, a chore which had entailed considerable risk since smallpox continuously killed more people about the city than Indians or outlaws ever did. During the month of May, 1882, fifteen cases were rampant about El Paso.[16]

Doc moved his family opposite the customshouse and opened an office in the Palace Drug Store.[17]

James, Frank and John Manning established a rustling empire, a business which started falling apart with the deaths of Campbell and Hale. Turning to other enterprises, they opened saloons, acquired real estate, and to a small extent become a political force. Jim pledged money and support for the El Paso *Times*[18] and even ran for mayor. He finished last in a field of four.[19]

The boys still managed to remain in trouble, however. On October 20, 1881, Sergeant Gillett arrested James and Frank Manning on a charge of assault with intent to kill. There are no details concerning this and apparently it amounted to very little.[20]

The Mannings were not without their champions. Coldwell, as mentioned, thought very highly of them and wrote: "Their general quietness and politeness [was] sufficient warning to others to avoid either familiarity or provocation." Coldwell commented that the killing of Hale and Campbell did not ignite the feud between the brothers and Stoudenmire, but regrettably, he offered no opinion as to what might have caused the holocaust.

Frank apparently went into business first, building a dive called Frank's Saloon about five miles west of El Paso near the end of the Southern Pacific Railroad line, the *Times* describing it as "one of the handsomest saloons in the country [with a] fine stock of goods."[21]

Frank's establishment represented civilization. Visitors tumbled off the railroad coaches, bellied their way inside the saloon, and washed the sand out of their mouths while waiting for transportation to town. And that transportation was something to behold. "Coaches, lumbering wagons, and the odds and ends of all sorts of vehicles run almost hourly to the end of the track, bringing in crowds of new residents and visitors."[22]

As the railroad hewed and blasted its way into El Paso, Frank Manning changed with the era. He leased from Mrs. Juana Dowell the old Ben Dowell Saloon on El Paso Street, now the site of the Paso del Norte Hotel. One wing of the building became a barber shop, the other a bar and club room. Varieties of rare and domestic wine were sold. A large adobe wall and corrals stood at the saloon rear, an advertisement reading: "Fine new box-stalls, double and single—the best care taken of teams and stock."[23] Frank paid Mrs. Dowell $185 a month for the lease.[24]

Jim Manning desired a bar business also. In April of 1881, he and Ike Blum became proprietors of the Gem Saloon,[25] but the partnership did not work out. On November 25, with brother John Manning as saloon treasurer, Jim and J. A. McDaniel[26] leased the El Paso Hotel and commenced redesigning it. A new business house now arose in the city, a unique establishment popularly known as the Coliseum Saloon and Variety Theatre. Entertainment choices were unlimited. In any of its nine rooms, a lonesome male could drink, gamble, play keno (a form of gambling similar to bingo), watch a play, or visit the cribs. Out back corrals and stables were attached.

Located on the west side of El Paso Street across from the intersection of First, the Coliseum resembled a barn more than it did a playhouse. Yet the newspapers reported that groups of some of the most noted actors in the profession played there, the theatre having a "seating capacity of 1500 [and a] stage 30 feet by 40 feet with ample dressing rooms on either wing."

In addition to the gallery extending across in front of the auditorium, there were "carpeted private boxes with elegant lace curtains"[27] for those not wishing to be seen or who furnished their private entertainment. The theatre opened on Monday, December 15, 1881, with seven musicians and seven entertainers from Leadville, Colorado.[28]

Although men who run saloons and brothels cannot ordinarily be classified as quiet types, the Manning brothers might have been little more than footnotes to El Paso history had it not been for their running feud with Dallas Stoudenmire.

As the street killings continued to multiply, the situation daily grew more tense. Dallas drank heavily. Doc lay dead. There had been several attempts on Stoudenmire's life and more might arrive at any moment. The politicians were grumbling and talk drifted about that the marshal's resignation would be asked for. Trouble stemmed frequently from the rangers. On top of all these woes, Dallas was a freedom-loving tomcat who spent considerable portions of his time in the bordellos. Such wanderings may not have necessarily reflected an unhappy home life (whoredom was an established precedent among most of El Paso's married males), but this, plus his drinking, gave Belle little marital satisfaction.

When drinking, Dallas would taunt the Mannings by setting up targets where he had shot down Campbell and Hale. For those unfortunate enough to have missed his first performance, he would drunkenly enact the killings all over again.[29]

On January 21, 1882, Jim Manning called a general meeting of saloon owners to be held in the Coliseum. The published announcement read, "There will be business of importance to discuss." No doubt all this talking concerned the marshal. But it did little good; the situation continued to get worse.

Threats between the two factions became such a daily occurrence that the *Lone Star* on March 25, 1882, printed a LAW AND ORDER editorial. "The citizens of El Paso are today standing on a volcano," it cried. While the commentary mentioned no names, the editor made it plain that he had the local feud under discussion. "Our streets may be deluged with blood at any moment and it is with the object of arousing people to a realization of this fact that these lines are penned."

The *Lone Star* refused to discuss the causes of events even though the editor demanded that something be done. "Violence if allowed to break forth[can] only have the effect of paralyzing business and driving people from the city. Now is not the time to discuss the right or wrong of past issues. Tale bearers[and] agitators [must] be made to understand that their services are not wanted and their interference will not be permitted."

Pleading for the best men in the community to step forward and work to avert the coming tragedy, the editor stated that, "Cool heads, stout hearts, and clear understanding are needed at this moment."

The editorial produced the desired effect. Leaders in the community did mediate the dispute and after nearly three weeks of negotiations, a truce was signed on April 16 by both parties, formally ending the difficulties.[30]

> We the undersigned parties having this day settled all differences and unfriendly feelings existing between us, hereby agree that we will hereafter meet and pass each other on friendly terms, and that bygones shall be bygones, and that we shall never allude in the future to any past animosities that have existed between us.
>
> Witness   Signed
> R. F. Campbell   Dallas Stoudenmire
> J. F. Harrison   J. Manning
> F. V. Hogan   G. F. Manning
> J. P. Hague   Frank Manning

It is important to note that this was not the type of truce following which both parties shook hands and bought a round of drinks. It was merely an agreement to hate on more silent terms. Nothing had really been settled.

chapter **11** STOUDENMIRE'S POLITICAL FEUD

DALLAS STOUDENMIRE had been hand-picked by the mayor and city council to be El Paso's peace officer, but it seemed obvious from the beginning that the marshal never had their full support. Alderman James Hague proved a good example. He voted against the original appointment on the grounds that Stoudenmire had not satisfied all the bond requirements. Although this criticism amounted to very little in the beginning, many of the politicians came to resent Stoudenmire's position and reputation. A few even feared him.

Dallas served early notice that he—not the politician—was marshal. A majority of the aldermen accepted this and did not interfere; others felt they had experience the marshal could profit by. One of these advisers was Noah H. Flood, a Kentuckian by birth who had served four terms as District Prosecuting Attorney for San Francisco.[1] Upon his election to the El Paso City Council in 1881, Flood surmised that one of his duties should be instructing the marshal in big city law enforcement. His intentions may have been honorable, but Stoudenmire wasn't paying any attention. Flood had barely hooked his thumbs in his vest and propped his foot against the jail bars when Dallas spun him around and drop-kicked him through the open door.[2] A dangerous enemy had been made, one more than Stoudenmire could afford.

Many of the politicans resented Stoudenmire, not because of what he had accomplished but because of the position he held. They shook their heads sadly at the thought of a common gunman in office. To a politician, the marshal's job meant a political power base.

Lusting after the office came W. W. Mills, a land-owner, financier, soldier of fortune, politician, United States Deputy Marshal, and one of the most intriguing and equally contrary scalawags ever to salt Texas with profanity. His book *Forty Years in El Paso* is primarily a tirade against his enemies (Stoudenmire included), although it is generally recognized as having astonishing insight concerning early El Paso.[3]

The marshal's office was a segment of the political spoils systems and a lawman existed only by the whim of the city council. Stoudenmire, however, managed to hang on when a dozen others would have been discharged. He was not discharged simply because he stood almost alone between law enforcement and chaos. Still, after each city election, the marshal had to be reappointed; and always standing along the sidelines loomed W. W. Mills, patiently waiting to submit his own name. The right time arrived on Ausust 30, 1881, immediately after Joseph Magoffin had been sworn in as mayor.

Mills' contrariness prevented him from becoming marshal. He simply could not muster enough popular support. But he tried and he exhibited a numerously signed petition recommending him for the office. Mills felt certain that the council would do the right thing.

In this case, however, Dallas Stoudenmire proved to be the more astute politician. He submitted his own petition, signed by seventy-three citizens, and the council bowed to this evidence of high esteem. Alderman Hague, in an effort to atone for trying to prevent Stoudenmire's initial appointment, offered the nomination. The marshal was voted unanimously back into office.[4]

Stoudenmire's popularity never soared any higher

than this. He had the support of the town and apparently the aldermen. This appointment proved to be the summit of his career. He had crested; his prestige would now begin to sink.

No difficulty became so great that he couldn't find an excuse to get drunk, or perhaps the difficulties furnished the excuses. He even tangled with Parson Tays.

The Reverend Mr. Tays had built the first protestant church in El Paso. There was nothing of the "Wild West" about the parson; he didn't carry a gun and he didn't preach in saloons. With his neatly combed gray beard, conventional black coat, and gold-headed black walking stick, the reverend gentleman was as much respected by the gamblers as he was by the average parishioner.

Ordinarily his sermons were modest affairs that offended no one. One Sunday morning, however, he preached an eloquent discourse which reflected on the drinking habits of Marshal Stoudenmire. When the news flew back to Dallas, he reacted as if the parson had broken one of his bottles. That night the marshal, in his usual liquored condition, left the Acme Saloon on San Antonio Street, turned the corner on what later became Mesa Avenue and stalked with a heavy tread up to the Church of St. Clements between Texas and Mills. Pulling both his six-shooters, he fired twelve bullets at the steeple bell.

Upon hearing the fusillade and the violent clanging, practically the entire population of El Paso jumped out of bed thinking the town was aflame. Fire alarms were usually given by a series of revolver shots, and this, combined with the ringing of the bell, made everyone believe that the blaze must be a large one.[5]

The marshal's drunken onslaughts against the peace and tranquility of the town were becoming an embarrassment to the city council. Aldermen met and agreed that an ordinance forbidding any public official to get drunk might act as a deterrent upon the marshal and tactfully hint that he was drifting out of bounds.

Of course they did not wish to make it appear that the law aimed itself solely at him, so they clothed the ruling in language calculated to remind the marshal that the council was concerned about everyone. On December 10, 1881, with Dallas Stoudenmire not in attendance,[6] the following resolution was adopted: "Any officer of the city of El Paso, who within the limits of said city be guilty of drunkenness, shall be fined not less than ten nor more than one hundred dollars." A list of city officers followed the ordinance, Stoudenmire's name falling a considerable way down the column.

Feeling good over all the sin they were abolishing, the aldermen decided to go further and make it unlawful for a citizen to carry a gun, fight, drink, gamble, swear, disturb the peace, expose himself indecently, or be "seen in the company of a known prostitute not his wife or some other relative."[7]

Naturally, both ordinances were ignored. It was still a common sight to witness the marshal wandering drunkenly through the streets. Often he did a little target practice at items which aroused his interest, and after expending ammunition and cussing for awhile, he would stagger home and settle into slumber.

The council rapidly ran out of patience. On March 25, 1882, the official minutes noted that Marshal Stoudenmire lay sick and unable to appear for work. Actually, everyone knew that he was sobering up from an acute case of the alcoholic jitters The following resolution was introduced and passed: "Whereas it has been made known to the city council of El Paso that the marshal is sick, confined to bed, and unable from this cause to do and perform his duties . . . that James B. Gillett . . . is hereby authorized and designated as the suitable and proper Assistant Marshal to take charge of the police force of this city, and so remain in charge until further orders and action of this council . . . and . . . that Dallas Stoudenmire be furnished a copy hereof, for his information."[8]

About the second or third of April, Marshal Stoudenmire was permitted to resume his duties. Immediately an old enemy chose this moment to try to unseat him. W. W. Mills, the man possessing unfailing delusions of leadership, submitted on April 5 the following statement addressed to the city council:[9]

Sir:

As a citizen I desire to state that I am informed and believe that the city marshal has vacated his office by accepting an appointment and qualifying as a Deputy United States Marshal. I give this information that your honorable body may take such action as you deem necessary and proper.

Stoudenmire was asked if this statement were true and he replied that it was not. He remarked that he had held such a position under Marshal Sherman, it being merely an authorization for him to carry a six-shooter in the territory of New Mexico. "I understood that my commission had lapsed," he said.

Alderman Hague insisted that the communication be given to the city attorney for an opinion. Mills was requested to furnish more information.

At the April 8 meeting Mills handed the council a telegram dated that very day and sent from Santa Fe, New Mexico, by Marshal John Sherman: "Dallas Stoudenmire is a United States Deputy Marshal for the Third Judicial District."

A committee now took the matter under advisement for possible action. Mayor Magoffin promised he would telegraph Sherman for more details.

At the next meeting, on April 13, Sherman's reply to Magoffin's query was read, although no notes appear in the minutes as to what it said. Apparently it merely supported what was already known. A motion was made and seconded that the office of city marshal be declared vacant. Voting was unanimous.

Alderman Hague then nominated W. W. Mills as the new city marshal, and the motion received a second. Alderman Schuster now rose and nominated Dallas Stoudenmire and his motion also got a second. The council stood deadlocked, two to two. Mayor Magoffin broke the tie by voting for Stoudenmire. Dallas found himself in office, thrown out, then voted back in again—all within a matter of minutes.[10]

As for Mills, he appeared stunned by the mayor's unexpected decision, but hid his disappointment by commenting that the vote came as a suprise to others also. According to his own account, he strove to rise above any pettiness, but Stoudenmire still bore him a grudge. One night during a public meeting at the Central Hotel, Stoudenmire accosted Mills, cursed him, and invited him to draw his weapons. Mills replied that he was unarmed and Dallas graciously offered to lend him a pistol. The offer received a quick refusal.[11]

Although the question of city marshal seemed settled, the council and Stoudenmire enjoyed no second honeymoon. Evidently the council had voted Dallas back into office to give him one more chance, an opportunity to redeem himself.

Every Monday morning the marshal rendered to the mayor a complete statement of fines collected by him—and then turned the money over to the city. Yet Stoudenmire stayed badly in arrears, so much so that he had not drawn a salary in three months. Newspapers happily pointed out that Assistant Marshal Gillett turned over large amounts of cash, while his boss had submitted almost nothing. By April 8, the mayor and Stoudenmire had spent days attempting to straighten out the account, although Dallas claimed that he had been ready to settle for weeks and the mayor had been putting him off. The *Lone Star* remarked that quite a sum of money was due, the implication being that the silver had financed Stoudenmire's frequent bouts with the bottle.[12]

Editor Carrico of the El Paso *Times* noted an increase in crimes of violence while Stoudenmire wrestled with the demons. He editorialized that while Dallas spreed, the outlawry rate tended to soar; when he was sober, a condition occurring with less and less frequency, the town slumbered quietly.

These editorials did not help the marshal's temper any, and he once stormed angrily into Carrico's office and threatened to run the newspaperman out of town. Carrico was far from being intimidated. He promptly raced to the city council and added his ringing voice to the chorus clamoring for Dallas Stoudenmire's discharge.[13]

The *Lone Star* also jumped into the fray. Editor Newman showed no concern about Stoudenmire's threat to run Carrico out of town; he would have been pleased at that happy turn of events. He exhibited concern, however, about the impending trouble between Stoudenmire and the Manning brothers, this only a week prior to the signing of the truce. An editorial was seared onto paper and aimed directly at the city council:

> The citizens of El Paso look for you to avert . . . the danger
> to the peace and prosperity of this city. Already the cloud
> that has been hanging over the community has seriously
> damaged every branch of business in the city; and an actual
> outbreak will retard the city a year in its growth. Every
> man, woman, and child in El Paso [is interested] in seeing
> quiet maintained. It is money in all our pockets. The

dullness of business at the present time is in great measure
due to the fact that many people outside have heard of the
troubles here and have been deterred from coming in and
not a few who were here have left. The council can, by
simply doing its plain duty, avert disaster and revive
business. That duty is to make a proper investigation of
both sides of the question, to do this with open doors, and
then remove or reinstate the marshal at once ... for the
best interests of the city. If he has not done his duty, or if
his continuance in office is a threat to the peace of the city,
he ought to be removed. Public policy dictates that, even if
a man be a good officer, if he be obnoxious in the
community, or if his continuance in office is liable to
provoke serious trouble, perhaps even a riot, he ought to be
removed. The safety of the community is of greater
moment than the personal interest of any individual. Let
the council act only from a high sense of public duty and
quit dilly-dallying. Either reinstate the Marshal at once and
thus show that he has not forfeited your confidence, or else
remove him and show that he has. In a word, do your duty,
and do it with open doors. The public will sustain you in it,
but they will never sustain you in the discussion of public
matters in secret session; and whatever you do, do it in such
a way to show that you are not working in the interest of
one faction at the expense of the other.

The editorial did not get the marshal removed, but his
days in office were plainly numbered; everyone, especially Dallas, knew
it. The council lacked the courage to discharge him, however, so the
matter drifted, the aldermen hoping that the marshal would take the
hint and resign.

Dallas Stoudenmire did not prove to be of a
suggestible nature. Finally on May 27, 1882, the council met to ask for
his resignation.[14] The meeting took place in Tivoli Hall, where the
council chambers were located. Tension hung heavy all day and some of
the aldermen were concerned about making it home alive that night.
Consequently, most of them sat in the enormous windows which
extended nearly to the ground, the excuse being that they needed the
cool night air. Not mentioned was that this position offered the fastest
escape from the chambers in case the marshal became violent.

One of the councilmen, Noah Flood, even entered the
building by the window route. Outside, he cautiously placed a shotgun
where he could reach it easily.

Alderman Phillips did not even attend, Judge Blacker saying in later years that "Since Stoudenmire had remarked that he would shoot Phillips on sight, his absence was perhaps not strange."[15]

Stoudenmire had been drinking heavily all day; he knew what the councilmen wanted and the knowledge did nothing to mollify his surly disposition. He had no sooner entered the chambers than he started growling threats and twirling his guns. Aldermen began squirming uneasily in their window seats.

Swearing and threatening, Marshal Stoudenmire paced around the room several times. Once he halted in front of Flood, a man of commanding appearance himself, and snapped, "I can straddle every God-damn alderman in this council." Nobody said a word.

Mayor Magoffin, realizing that this was not the day to discuss a dismissal, declared an adjournment until the following Monday. Dallas left the building without knowing that Flood had a shotgun.

On Monday, May 29, the marshal had calmed down. He was also sober and had his resignation written out:[16]

> Believing as I do that under the present administration of the city government my usefulness as city marshal will become materially impaired and learning that there will be an attempt to reduce the pay of the marshal, already too low, I hereby tender my resignation as city marshal. Before parting company with the officers of the city, while I feel that I have suffered an injustice from certain members of your honorable body, I think it is my duty to, and do hereby, apologize for my conduct in the council chamber last Saturday evening and beg to assure you that I meant no disrespect to your body or the people whom you represent.

After listening to the resignation, the city fathers decided to forget the past. Alderman Hague rose and made a speech applauding the marshal's faithful service and offered several resolutions which praised his competent discharge of duties in the "dangerous and difficult position he . . . held in our midst."

Alderman Blacker then offered a few moderate resolutions and the order of business turned to selecting a new marshal. Ben Schuster nominated James B. Gillett and the assistant marshal was approved unanimously.

El Paso drew a long breath now that the crisis had passed. The *Lone Star* felt "highly gratified by this action of the city fathers and the city is to be congratulated at the happy termination of affairs which has been a standing menace to the peace and good name of El Paso."[17]

Texas Rangers were elated also. Captain Baylor wrote General King, saying, "Stoudenmire greatly to my relief having resigned after bullying the mayor and council, Gillett has been made marshal so that a legal mob is now in office. You should have no more gripes about me."[18]

Most of El Paso felt that with Dallas Stoudenmire's retirement the danger of bloodshed was averted. Actually when his star was thrown down, the restraints were off and the spectre of sudden death loomed larger.

chapter **12**   PRELUDE TO A GUNFIGHT

A FTER DALLAS Stoudenmire's resignation, he continued to loll around town and live on the earnings of the Globe Restaurant which Doc had left him.[1] If the revenue from the dining hall was not great, it at least provided him with enough money for drinks and the other necessities of life.

Dallas bore no bitter feelings toward Jim Gillett for inheriting the job of city marshal. Perhaps it was because Jim had no small reputation himself and appeared unafraid of Stoudenmire. At any rate, Stoudenmire warmly congratulated Gillett and promised his help if it should ever be needed.

On July 13, 1882, United States Marshal Hal L. Gosling appointed Dallas Stoudenmire a Deputy United States Marshal for the western district of Texas, with headquarters in El Paso.[2]

That Dallas served now as a deputy marshal did not deter Gillett from enforcing the city ordinances impartially. Like his former boss, Gillett had learned his trade well and practiced no favoritism. Before long he was obliged to discipline his earlier supervisor.

Stoudenmire as usual managed to remain in trouble. On July 29, Billy Bell and William Page, the latter one of Stoudenmire's former assistant city marshals, got into an altercation at the Acme Saloon and Dallas happened upon the scene. He grabbed Page about the body and half-carried, half-pushed him to Doyle's Concert Hall. There he and Page started drinking heavily and left about midnight, returning to the Acme, where they commenced to quarrel. Dallas attempted to resolve the disp te in a hurry and permanently. He jerked one of his pistols and shot at Page who, sobering fast, knocked Stoudenmire's gun-hand up into the air just as the weapon discharged. The bullet thudded into the ceiling. Then, taking a firm grip on Stoudenmire's pistol, Page tore it away from him.

Dallas now drew his second revolver and, glancing down the barrel, prepared to send Page to Concordia Cemetery. Just then the ex-city marshal noticed a movement at his side and, glancing around, found himself staring into the twin barrels of a shotgun held in the firm hands of Marshal Gillett. Page and Stoudenmire were both arrested and fined $25 each the next morning in court.[3] In addition, Dallas was placed under a $250 peace bond.[4]

Much of Deputy Marshal Stoudenmire's work kept him in the territory of New Mexico, but he still thought of El Paso and fumed about his troubles there. Once that summer he rode a train from Albuquerque to Las Vegas, New Mexico, sitting in the same car and chatting with the famed New Mexico Sheriff Pat Garrett. Both Stoudenmire and Garrett were guests of Fred Leach, Superintendent of the lower division of the Santa Fe Railroad. Leach, according to a gentlemen who knew all the parties, had frequently employed both lawmen in the prevention and detection of train robberies and the arresting of outlaws.[5]

Everyone took another train at Las Vegas and traveled a short distance to Hot Springs, where the railroad maintained several hotels and bathhouses.

Stoudenmire looked haggard and nervous from the effects of one long drinking spree, his hand shaking so badly that others had to sign his name on the register at the Montezuma Hotel. That afternoon he took a hot bath and, feeling better, he consented to speak to several admirers who clustered about him:

"I was pretty nigh single handed against the town [El Paso] and everybody trying to get the drop on me to kill me. It got so that if a man had a charge in his gun that he wanted to get rid of, he'd wait around the corner and fire it into me. I don't mind a shooting scrape when it comes; it was the suspense that wore on me. I never knew when I might be attacked unawares. It might happen in a railroad train or anywhere that I chance to be. I've had the offer of two different city marshalships this week. I don't know what I'll do about them. Go back to El Paso maybe when I get straightened up."

Someone asked what he felt about death: "I believe that when a man is born, the time when he is to die is fixed and appointed and he can't be killed before that time comes around. I don't believe the bullet was ever molded that will kill me."[6]

When Stoudenmire left Hot Springs, he had regained much of his old bounce and happy-go-lucky nature. He was exercising and looked in excellent physical shape. Then during a period of conversation with Marshal Gosling, Dallas spoke of his troubles with the Manning brothers and others in El Paso. Gosling listened quietly and then advised Stoudenmire to meet once again with his enemies and discuss the feud. Stoudenmire agreed and, since he had to serve a warrant in El Paso, he told Marshal Gosling that he would begin anew the process of peace talks.

On Sunday night, September 17, 1882, about eleven o'clock, Dallas Stoudenmire, who had been consuming liquor all day, was poured off the Deming,[7] New Mexico, train at El Paso. Brushing his pants, he staggered toward the center of town and his destiny. In his shirt pocket he carried a warrant for an unknown party, a warrant which was to play an important role in his destiny that very night. His first stop was the Acme Saloon, where he consumed several glasses of whiskey.

"Why don't you go home and get in bed?" C. C. Brooks, the bartender and one of the three owners, queried.

"No, I'm not going home; in fact, I'm going to stay up all night. Why don't you close and come down to some of the houses with me?"

"You are drinking and I won't do it," Brooks answered.

"Well," Dallas replied, "I am going across the street. I suppose you will be open when I come back."[8] He pushed his frame through the doors and stepped out into the night.

Stoudenmire walked past the Cobweb Saloon and hesitated in front of Frank Manning's place where, fingering the warrant, he paused briefly to peer inside. The wanted man was not there.

Dallas turned without entering and strolled back to the Acme Saloon where Brooks stood counting the day's receipts, preparatory to closing. Sitting down, the deputy marshal poured himself another drink. As he took the glass from his lips, an intoxicated Mexican named Tom Ochoa staggered in and demanded that Stoudenmire arrest a stranger who had threatened his life. Dallas merely glanced up without speaking and finally Brooks warned Tom to be silent, following his remarks by expelling the drunk from the premises.[9]

When the Acme closed, Brooks changed his mind and sauntered with Stoudenmire down to Abbie Bell's parlor house. Together they stood in the yard while Dallas called drunkenly for Carrie, his favorite. The madam, Abbie Bell, charged outside to suppress the noise and inform Dallas that Carrie had gone uptown for a bite to eat. Dallas decided to wait in the parlor; Brooks went home. The time read three o'clock in the morning.

Prostitution in El Paso was in its embryonic stage during Stoudenmire's time, but it served its purpose. The madams were learning and developing the flamboyance which would characterize their operations in later years. While he waited for Carrie, Dallas could relax in a comfortable chair, probably red plush, and pour his troubles into the ear of an attentive bosomy maiden.

Any girl in any of the bordellos had heard more sides to any political controversy than any helpmate in town. It was small wonder she make her listening a solacing comfort and her nodding agreement a bolster to the male ego. A man could walk out feeling ten feet tall, or he could spend the venom accumulated during a day's association with the work-a-day world in a spasm of forgetfulness and sink into peaceful oblivion.

No records identify Abbie Bell or even the location of her bordello. As for Carrie, she could have been any one of a hundred working girls who plied their trade in the long row of houses. The place was obviously well above the cribs, where girls sat in open windows with their legs cocked at inviting angles and called to potential customers who passed along the streets. Some of the harlots hung over the lower half of Dutch doors, giving the goggling clientele a good view of the upper portion of their anatomies, while snagging strangers by the arms when they passed too close. And if business got really bad, the girls trotted right out into the road and dragged their prey inside.

As city marshal, Dallas had had the opportunity to practice comparative shopping among El Paso's love stores, since he was responsible for collecting fines and license fees and maintaining law and order. He knew the merchandise, so he waited for Carrie to return from her "lunch break."

Stoudenmire interrupted the march of destiny by whiling away the early morning hours with Carrie. History does not record whether he made it home that night or whether he spent his remaining hours of peace at Abbie Bell's parlor house. He later said he had plenty of sleep.

chapter **13** A GUNFIGHT AT
FRANK MANNING'S SALOON

Dallas Stoudenmire's brief pause to peer into Frank Manning's Saloon to look for a wanted man was the act which had triggered the events to come. A person whom the El Paso *Herald* referred to as a "superserviceable individual" had noticed Dallas glancing into the establishment. He went straightway to warn the Brothers Manning that Stoudenmire was looking for them. While Dallas was partaking of Carrie's charms, the Mannings were arming and preparing for trouble.

It was noon of the following day, September 18, before Dallas Stoudenmire put in an appearance. He walked lightly into the Acme Saloon, nodded to Brooks, and took a chair at the rear. A few minutes later Frank Manning walked in. He was in his shirt sleeves and wearing a vest; a forty-five sagged noticeably at his hip.

"How about a drink?" Frank said. Brooks grabbed a bottle and poured two.

"How about another?" Frank remarked again. Brooks complied.

While they talked, Dallas walked behind the bar.

Without speaking, he picked up a bottle and glass. Drinking silently, he finally turned away to a table and sat down about twenty feet from Manning.

"I am damn sorry to see this thing happen," Brooks said to Frank.

"Brooks, it is not my fault," Frank replied. "I have tried every way to keep this thing down. You know what happened last night."

"I don't want any trouble in my saloon," Brooks snapped.

"I would just as soon it happen here as in the hills or any place else," Frank said. "The sooner it comes off, the better for all parties."

Stoudenmire rose and passed outside, strolling within shoulder-rubbing distance of Frank Manning. Neither man moved over an inch.

With Dallas gone, Frank walked into the gambling room, only to return in a few minutes and say, "Brooks, I am the last man in the world to raise any disturbance. I am not going to bother anybody if they will leave me alone."

The doorway darkened as Stoudenmire stepped back into the room and seated himself at the rear of the saloon. Following close behind came Dr. Manning, who took a chair near the billiard table. Upon being offered a drink by Brooks, Doc stepped up to the bar and stood beside his brother.

Stoudenmire's face showed a sour expression as he watched his hated enemies. In disgust, he left. After he disappeared, the Mannings went outside, stood there talking among themselves for fifteen minutes, then drifted away.

Dallas strolled into the Gem Saloon where his hangover began showing improvement. He literally sprang through the portals and sang a silly song as he entered. Dancing along the bar, he stopped beside A. L. Nichols, the druggist, to make reference to the Mannings. "Them sons of bitches have put up a job to kill me this evening."

Speaking more to himself than anyone else, he muttered that he might be drunk, but he had plenty of sleep and considered himself "a match for them fellows at any time."[1]

Nichols tried to talk him into going home, but the deputy marshal merely ignored the advice, stuck a cigar in his mouth, and headed for the Pony Saloon. Another man came in as Dallas went out and he told Nichols that papers were being sworn out for Stoudenmire's arrest.[2] The druggist hurried to notify Dallas of this and Stoudenmire indicated that he would go over to Judge Blacker's office and smooth the situation over.

Instead of visiting the Judge, however, he bumped into J. W. Jones, another owner of the Acme. During the street conversation, Dallas told Jones that he desired no trouble with the Mannings. He explained that he had not been searching for the brothers the night before, but had only been trying to serve a warrant. "I want no trouble," Stoudenmire said, "but if they are bound to fight, I will fight any one of them." Jones was requested to convey this message to the Mannings.

Jones passed the information on to Bartender Brooks, who took it to the brothers. They seemed relieved to hear that Dallas was not applying his warpaint. They sought no killing either. Frank in particular suffered from a premonition of death, and he appeared especially glad to hear that the incident would be allowed to pass over. He mentioned that "his brothers were all married and had children, and if he were killed his brothers would be the only ones who would grieve over him."[3]

Brooks continued to carry the peace pipe back and forth between the two warring factions, and it finally appeared that arrangements for a new truce were all but settled. Only whiskey was needed to seal the agreement. At about five-thirty that evening Stoudenmire asked Brooks and Jones to accompany him to Frank Manning's Saloon where everyone would take a drink and shake hands.

Brooks went inside the saloon first, closely followed by Stoudenmire and Jones. Jim stood near the bar; Dr. Manning was playing billiards. Everyone spoke pleasantly. To a stranger, it could have been a gathering of close friends.

Walking up to the bar, Dallas said, "Come up, Doc, and have a drink." Then he asked where Frank was.

"I don't know," Jim replied, "but I'll go see if I can

find him." He left.

Now Dr. Manning stepped up to the bar where he and Stoudenmire stood side by side. Dallas turned to face him, saying, "Some liars or damn sons of bitches have been lying on both parties and have been trying to make trouble."

"Dallas, you haven't stuck to the terms of your agreement," the doctor snapped.

"Whoever says I have not tells a damn lie!"

Jones jumped between the two men and pushed them apart, an extremely brave act, one which cost Stoudenmire precious time. Off balance, Dallas became the last to draw. Before he could swing his gun clear from what is believed to have been a left-handed cross-draw, Dr. Manning started shooting over the shoulder of Jones who had crouched down. Doc's first shot smashed through Stoudenmire's left arm, severed an artery, glanced off and entered the chest, struck a rib and exited through the breast. Stoudenmire's pistol which he had half-drawn, went spinning across the room.

Dallas gasped and reeled backwards, closely pursued by Dr. Manning. As Stoudenmire slammed into the door, he was shot again. This time the doctor's firing pin struck upon a faulty cartridge containing a weak powder charge. Even then, damage was done as the bullet smashed into Stoudenmire's chest and kicked the breath from him in a blood-frothing grunt.

Although the slug knocked him completely outside the saloon, it was found later that the ball had struck a thick wad of papers in his shirt pocket, probably tore through the warrant, and lodged in his shirt. A case holding the picture of an unidentified woman (probably his sister Virginia) also helped stop the bullet.

Dr. Manning tumbled nearly on top of Stoudenmire as the two gladiators fought their way outside. By this time however, Stoudenmire had managed to draw his pocket pistol and he fired as Doc jumped out on the sidewalk. The slug struck Manning in the right arm between the elbow and shoulder, inflicting an excruciating wound and causing Doc's weapon to fly out into El Paso Street.

Had Stoudenmire not been so badly shot up, the fight would have ended immediately. But he reeled with physical anguish and the doctor was close upon him, so close that he rushed the big man, gripped him tightly about the body and arms, and began to grapple. This action effectively prevented Dallas from getting off another shot.

As the two men banged along the walkway between the adobe gallery supports and the wall, struggling and cursing, Dallas trying to kill and the doctor trying desperately to stay alive, Jim Manning came rushing up. Pulling a concealed .45 with a missing trigger and a sawed off barrel,[4] he thumbed the hammer once and fired at Stoudenmire's bobbing and weaving head. The bullet missed and smashed a barber pole.

Jim stepped closer, to a distance of about eight feet from the two men. He shot again and Stoudenmire groaned as the bullet struck him an inch above and slightly to the rear of the left ear. His revolver slipped into the dirt from blood-drenched hands and the tall man stretched out in death.

chapter **14** END OF AN ERA

A S DALLAS Stoudenmire gasped and died, onlookers came scurrying out of the niches where they had sought refuge during the fusillade.[1] Marshal Gillett, who had been standing in Kaplan's store on El Paso Street, approached just in time to assist Rangers J. M. Deaver and Ed Scotten in pulling Dr. Felix Manning off Stoudenmire's inert body. Sitting astride his dead enemy, the doctor was wildly battering Stoudenmire across the head with the deputy marshal's own pistol.[2]

Gillett placed Jim and Doc Manning under arrest and turned the prisoners over to Assistant Marshal Comstock. In the confusion, he took as evidence the guns of both Stoudenmire and Dr. Manning, but Jim Manning's weapon was not confiscated.

"Help me get my brother inside, " Jim pleaded. "I think he is killed." The slightly built doctor was then carefully picked up and taken to the back room of the Manning saloon, where his shattered arm was bandaged.

A coroner's jury was hastily assembled and several pages of testimony were written down, none of which has been preserved except for the newspaper versions. During the inquest an oddity occurred. Eyewitnesses testified that Jim Manning came running armed toward the struggle, that he pointed what looked like a gun at Stoudenmire, that a shot rang out and smoke arose from this weapon and engulfed the scene—but no one would actually swear that Jim Manning had anything to do with the slaying. As a result, the hearing ended with the remarkable verdict that "Dallas Stoudenmire on the evening of September 18, 1882, came to his death from a shot fired by a six-shooter .44 or .45 caliber in the hands of party unknown."[3]

The El Paso district attorney would not accept the findings of the inquest. In October the following indictments were drawn up:[4]

> Felix Manning unlawfully, feloniously, and of his malice aforethought, made an assault upon Dallas Stoudenmire with the unlawful and felonious intent to murder.

> James Manning did unlawfully, feloniously, and with malice aforethought kill and murder Dallas Stoudenmire by shooting the said Dallas Stoudenmire with a pistol.

As expected, the trials were short and the outcome a foregone conclusion. In separate trials the brothers were found not guilty. Dr. Manning did not even show up for his day in court. W. R. Hall, an army surgeon, certified on October 23 that Felix lay under his care for a gunshot wound in the right arm involving injury to a nerve. "He [Dr. Manning] has neuralgia of great severity [and] is unfit to appear in court."

Interestingly enough, the foreman of the jury which acquitted Dr. Manning was W. W. Mills, Stoudenmire's old enemy! On the jury which acquitted Jim Manning was Ike Blum, Jim's old business partner in the Gem Saloon!

The Manning brothers did not find life easy after the death of Dallas Stoudenmire. It seems that with Dallas gone, they had little left to do. Within two years all were gone from El Paso.

John Manning, the only brother who does not seem to have been deeply involved in the power struggle with Dallas Stoudenmire, was appointed an El Paso County deputy sheriff in the early part of 1883. About this time, Sheriff Gonzales was anxious to resign and John Manning felt sure that he was a shoo-in for the position.

John had enemies, however, and they managed to circumvent his best-laid plans. Other powerful elements were pushing James H. White and White finally won out. In frustration, John became an El Paso assistant marshal, serving only a few months before Hal Gosling appointed him a Deputy United States Marshal. Now some interesting things began to happen. On October 31, 1883, John Manning's former county activities caught up with him and he was charged in three indictments (later dropped to two indictments) with swindling and misapplication of county funds.[5]

Regardless of whether or not the charges were ever proved, John Manning still worked for Uncle Sam who—then as now—had a generous and forgiving heart.

On February 10, 1885, United States Marshal Hal and Deputy Marshals John Manning and Fred Loring were transporting two convicted stagecoach robbers by train. The prisoners, James Pitts and Charles Yeager, had been tried in Austin, Texas, sentenced to life imprisonment, and were being taken to the San Antonio jail prior to confinement in Huntsville.

On board the same train were the prisoners' wives, mothers, sisters, and male friends. In an explosive situation such as that, the marshals unbelievably blundered. They hancuffed the two criminals together and installed them in a seat two or three rows back of the officers and across the aisle.

Near New Braunsfels, Pitts' mother-in-law and Yeager's sister walked down the passageway, paused for a minute or two beside their relatives, and sauntered on. Seconds later, the convicts rose from their seats, slipped up behind the unobservant officers, and commenced firing. Gosling fell dead in the lap of John Manning, a bullet through his head and several in his body. Manning took two slugs in his left shoulder and one in the neck, causing him to fall out into the aisle. Loring was apparently answering a call of nature in another part of the train since he was not shot nor did he return any of the gunfire. As the prisoners backed from the car, shooting as they went, John Manning struggled from the floor, and fired a rapid volley of shots at the two men. However, the escapees made it to the rear platform, where they jumped. There Pitts fell to the ground and moaned, "Oh Lord, how that little Manning peppered me. I'm full of holes." He died about two hundred yards from the track.[6]

Fred Loring gathered a posse in the next town and Yeager was soon captured. As for John Manning, he slowly recovered from his wounds, resigned, and drifted off to Washington state to live. All efforts to trace him have come to naught.[7]

In November of 1882, it was found that Bill Thompson, brother to the notorious Ben Thompson, had been hiding in El Paso for several months in an effort to remain out of a Corpus Christi jail. He was captured, however, and ordered to be returned and face a murder charge. By some quirk of frontier logic, Frank Manning, who admitted being a close friend of Thompson's, was chosen to escort the prisoner back to the Gulf Coast city. As expected, Bill Thompson escaped in route.[8]

By even more fantastic frontier logic, this escapade helped qualify Frank Manning to become the new El Paso City Marshal who, on April 18, 1883, replaced James Gillett.

Frank's tenure of office proved to be nearly as unhappy as Dallas Stoudenmire's. On May 26, Marshal Manning entered the store of Mr. Walz and made a demand which Walz refused to honor. Frank became enraged, seized the storekeeper by the shirt, cursed him, hit him over the head with a heavy cane, and pushed him into a back office, where he threatened him with a revolver.[9]

Not satisfied that he had himself in enough trouble, Frank Manning now hunted up Deputy Assessor Stromblatt, slapped his face, shoved a pistol under his nose and challenged him to go to Mexico with him and see who was the better man. Evidently the sole difficulty between the two men was Stromblatt's refusal to advance the candidacy of John Manning for sheriff. Stromblatt had unwisely allied himself with James White. At any rate, Stromblatt was fully aware of Frank Manning's dexterity with a gun and he declined the invitation to shoot it out in Old Mexico.[10]

A city-wide uproar now followed Frank Manning's footsteps and he swiftly resigned to avoid discharge.

From El Paso, Frank and brother James went to Arizona and mined for gold and silver—unsuccessfully. Dr. Manning decided to join them and he began his practice anew in Flagstaff.

As the years slipped by, Frank's mind lapsed into senility. Dr. Manning did his best to care for the brother, furnishing him a shed to live in at the rear of the doctor's house. But Frank existed for one pleasure, to prospect. He would saddle his burro and disappear into the mountains for weeks, once leaving a new pair of store bought-teeth on a rock out in the hills.[11] Finally Frank's mentality sagged so badly that the Manning family had him committed to the Arizona State Hospital in 1922. He died there on November 14, 1925.[12]

James Manning married Leonor Isabelle Arzate in El Paso, moved to Arizona where he prospected for a short time, and then took his family to Seattle, Washington, where he owned a liquor store. On June 6, 1889, a fire-storm gutted the entire business district of downtown Seattle and Jim, like everyone else, lost nearly everything.

Undaunted, he opened a saloon in Anacortes, Washington, and settled his family on Orcas Island. The business was unsuccessful and, nearly bankrupt, he journeyed to Las Angeles where he recouped part of his fortune and reinvested it in the copper and silver mines of Parker, Arizona.

Now began a very trying period of his life. The mines never paid off, and in despair Jim began spending less and less time with his family. He stayed in Arizona, arguing with his wife that the next strata of rock would bring an end to their financial misfortune. The hard work finally made him ill; the mines accomplishing what no gunman had ever been able to do. His wife borrowed money to return him to Las Angeles where he lingered for several months, slowly dying of cancer of the spleen and liver. An old bullet wound, never properly cared for, aggravated his condition. He died in April, 1915, and is buried in Forest Lawn cemetery.[13] Numerous descendants still reside in various portions of the West.

As for Doc Manning, he built a respectable life for himself in Flagstaff, dying there on March 9, 1925.[14] He too left children.

The final main character in the Stoudenmire drama was James B. Gillett. Marshal Gillett presided over a quiet El Paso after the death of Dallas Stoudenmire. Unlike his former boss, Gillett made peace with the Manning brothers. They presented him with a gold-plated badge on which was inscribed a shield, and on the shield were the words "City Marshal, El Paso, Texas." On the reverse side was the astonishing inscription "Presented by the Manning Brothers and Charlie Utter."[15]

The path of El Paso law enforcement did not always run smooth for Marshal James B. Gillett either. He allowed himself to become involved in an altercation with Mayor pro tem Paul Keating. A rumor, supposedly traced to Gillett, began circulating around that Keating was often too drunk to attend to his duties. This enraged Keating who promptly insinuated that Gillett had officially collected money without properly accounting for it.

Now Gillett grew indignant. He struck Keating several times with his fist, then pulled his gun and threatened to shoot him.

Keating promptly swore out a warrant for Marshal Gillett's arrest, charging "assault and battery and threats of shooting." Although in serious trouble, Gillett had the support of the town and probably could have survived the onslaught. He had been considering going into the ranching business however and chose this as a good time to resign.[16]

Gillett's first attempt at ranching proved to be a failure. A man named Tarde drove a herd of Mexican yearlings onto the range and within weeks the fever had claimed thirty-five head of Gilett's stock valued at $1,100.[17]

With his hat in his hand, Jim approached the city of El Paso for his old position as city marshal—but all that was open was an assistant marshal's position. He accepted this, served for a year or so, and resigned once more to enter the cattle business around Marfa, Texas. Here he got religion and became a leading speaker at cowboy camp meetings.[18] Death came in June, 1937.[19]

chapter 15 DAY OF JUDGEMENT

T HE BODY of Dallas Stoudenmire was lifted from the dirt and hauled to the undertaker's, where a decision pended on what to do with it. Belle wanted her husband buried in Columbus, Texas, but Stoudenmire's assets were negligible. The Freemasons, Lodge No. 130, A.F.&F.M., solved the difficulty when they met to pay final tribute to a deceased brother, Dallas Stoudenmire, who had received his third degree on January 7, 1882. John Denny, historian of freemasonry in El Paso, notes that "To afford his numerous friends an opportunity for seeing his remains for the last time, the lodge room remained open to the public until 6 p.m. Lumber for Stoudenmire's coffin cost the lodge $4.50 and his suit of burial clothes, $11.55."[1]

Dallas left no will. Like most gunfighters, he died with only the clothes on his back and a considerable body of debts. Virginia Cummings, his sister, told the probate court that she was his only living relative over twenty-one years old in the state and she would sell his possessions, collect what money he had coming from the United States government,[2] and pay off his creditors.[3]

Stoudenmire's body was shipped to Colorado

County, Texas, and lay in state at a hotel in Alleyton. Several friends
and relatives of the deceased and his wife spent a night's prayer vigil
around the casket.[4]

On the following day, September 23, the Masonic
Caledonia Lodge, No. 68, A.F.&F.M. of Columbus, buried him in the
cemetery at Alleyton.[5] At one time a large stone marked the location,
but it has since been destroyed and there is no way of locating the
exact site.[6]

Now that this particular epoch has passed, who is to
say that Dallas Stoudenmire was not El Paso's man on horseback? In his
own way he was a pioneer; and pioneers are unorthodox people,
dynamic and domineering, imperfect and veined with human flaws, at
times able to fire the thoughts and control the destinies of others, but
rarely able to salvage any sort of comfortable life for themselves.

Above all, pioneers are rebels; and the line which
separates public heroes from those who are hanged is very fine and
sometimes wavy.

Stoudenmire's popularity has not been large due to a
brief life and little press-agentry. Had it not been for the burst of
shooting which sank Johnny Hale and George Campbell in death, he
might never have been remembered at all except as a drunken footnote
in Western history—just another gunman who found himself crossways
in the liquor bottle.

A psychiatrist would say that Stoudenmire suffered
from deep feelings of inferiority. How else can one explain his bragging,
his bravado, his shooting at targets that represented victims, his heavy
drinking, and his quickness to take offense? Without these short-
comings he might have lived longer, but he would never have been as
interesting or as colorful.

Dallas imagined himself to be an outstanding pistol
shot, and he was above average—but never great. He matched himself
with an out-of-towner named Jones on August 6, 1882. The betting
soared to $100 on Dallas Stoudenmire, the favorite, and distances of
twenty-five to one hundred and fifty yards were marched off. Mesa
Gardens grew crowded that day; the whole town turned out to watch
and wager on the local champion. Yet, when the night closed down,
about half the city went home broke and disillusioned. Dallas

Stoudenmire had ingloriously lost. A few days later Dallas matched himself with Captain James H. White and again emerged on the humiliating end of an eight-to-two defeat.[7]

It could very well be that in a life full of many turning points, this became the most fateful one. He had finally come face to face with himself as a fallible gunman. Others realized this too, especially the Manning brothers. For the first time, they may have entertained thoughts that Stoudenmire could be beaten. Also, for the first time, Dallas may have begun to doubt his ability to conquer them in a fight. We saw an example of this when Stoudenmire sent word to the Mannings on the day of his death that he would scrap with any *one* of them at a time. Such a remarkable change in such a short time! In the old days, the marshal would have challenged them all immediately and called them out into the street.

Nevertheless, Dallas Stoudenmire should not be judged on the strength of his killings, his excessive drinking, or even the circumstances surrounding his death. When he came to El Paso, the village was just starting to move. It claimed newness at being respectable and so did he. Both he and the town and the Manning Brothers were trying to grow and all did the best they could in an atmosphere of change.

This is what should be remembered now that the gunsmoke has blown away.

The end.

FOOTNOTES

CHAPTER 1

1. See C. L. Sonnichsen, *Ten Texas Feuds,* University of New Mexico Press (Albuquerque, 1957), 108-156; *The El Paso Salt War,* Carl Hertzog and the Texas Western Press (El Paso, 1961).

2. The occupation of Woods is given in the local newspaper advertisement of the day.

3. El Paso Public Library, City Council Minutes, Typescript, Book 2, 22. Hereafter cited as City Council Minutes.

4. The occupation of Stevens is given by the 1880 census of El Paso County.

5. City Council Minutes, Book B, 37.

6. William M. Coldwell reviewing James B. Gillett's *Six Years With The Texas Rangers* for an El Paso newspaper.

7. James B. Gillett, *Six Years With the Texas Rangers,* Yale University Press (New Haven, 1925), 233. Young County has no available records indicating that Campbell ever served there in any official capacity. Mr. D. D. Cusenbary (Young County Treasurer) to L. C. M., August 12, 1966.

8. George W. Baylor to General King, September 30, 1881, Webb Texas Ranger Reports, University of Texas Archives. Hereafter cited as University Archives.

9. City Council Minutes, Book B, 56.

10. John B. Jones to Baylor, January 6, 1881, Adjutant General's File, Texas State Library, Austin. Hereafter cited as AGF.

11. Baylor to Jones, May 8, 1881, AGF.

12. Baylor to King, September 30, 1881, University Archives.

13. City Council Minutes, Book B, 68-71.

14. Gillett wrote two different versions of who was sent to El Paso. In his book *Six Years . . .* 233, he says that Baylor told him to go. However, in another writing, "The Killing of Dallas Stoudenmire,*"Frontier Times* (July 1924,) 24, he comments that Captain Baylor sent Corporal Jim Fitch. Baylor is responsible for the story of Gillett and Lloyd going. Baylor to King, September 30, 1881, University Archives.

15. Baylor to King, September 30, 1881, University Archives.

16. Baylor, "Record of Scouts," February 28, 1881, AGF.

17. *Ibid*, March 31, 1881.

18. *Ibid.*

19. Baylor to Capt. Neal Coldwell, April 5, 1881, AGF.

20. City Council Minutes, Book B. 94.

CHAPTER 2

1. Cleofas Calleros, *El Paso's Missions and Indians,* McMath Company (El Paso, 1951), 17.

2. El Paso *Times,* New Year's edition, 1882.

3. Colorado County *Citizen,* April 28, 1881.

4. Letter written by Charles Richardson to U. S. State Department, October 14, 1881. Microflim Copy 184 entitled "Dispatches from U. S. Consuls in Ciudad Juarez," Roll No. 2, Call Number 327.73097un3dj.

5. George Look manuscript.

6. Richardson, *op. cit.*

CHAPTER 3

1. Aberfoil is now in Bullock County.

2. Mrs. Alex Stoudenmire to LCM, August 19, 1966.

3. Carey E. Haigler to LCM, July 23, 1965. Mr. Haigler is a distant relative of Dallas Stoudenmire.

4. Mrs. Alex Stoudenmire to LCM, August 19, 1966.

5. James M. Black, *The Families and Descendants in America of Golsan, Golson, Gholson, and Gholston,* published by James M. Black (Salt Lake City, 1959), 459.

6. James M. Black to LCM February 10, 1966.

7. Mrs. Alex Stoudenmire to LCM, July 4, 1966.

8. James M. Black to LCM, April 12, 1966.

9. Mrs. Alex Stoudenmire to LCM, July 28, 1966.

10. Haigler to LCM, November 11, 1965.

11. *Ibid.,* September 12, 1965.

12. File Designation: Dallas Stoudenmire, Co. E, 45th Alabama Infantry, CSA, National Archives and Records Service, Washington, D.C.

13. *Ibid.*

14. *Ibid.*

15. El Paso *Herald,* April 19, 1882.

16. *Ibid.,* April 9, 1895.

17. Haigler to LCM, November 11, 1965. At least one of Dallas Stoudenmire's older brothers may have been killed during the Civil War. Meshak, who was married, moved to Montgomery, Alabama, and became a brick mason. On July 19, 1861, he enlisted in Co. B, 13 Alabama Infantry Regiment. Three months later on October 7, he lay dead of an undisclosed disease. Peter

Brannon, Director of Alabama Archives, to LCM, December 12, 1965. However, the Tennessee State Archives show a Meshak Stoudenmire enlisting in Co. K, 3rd Tennessee Cavalry on March 25, 1864. Mr. Walker M. Love, Senior Archivist, to LCM, February 2, 1966.

18. Nod Clapp, El Campo, Texas, telephone interview with LCM, November 27, 1965. Mr. Clapp remembered his mother's speaking of Dallas Stoudenmire and Colonel Stoudenmire.

19. Haigler to LCM, September 12, 1965.

20. Frank Manning, Tucson, Arizona, interview with C. L. Sonnichsen, El Paso, Texas November 5, 1965. Mr. Manning knew very little about and expressed some uncertainty about this phase of Doc Manning's career.

21. Dallas Stoudenmire, Texas Ranger Muster Rolls, AGF.

22. John B. Jones to Headquarters Frontier Battalion, May 7, 1874, General Order No. 1, University Archives.

23. Jones to Steele, September 20, 1874, University Archives.

24. Texas Ranger Muster Rolls, AGF.

25. Colorado County *Citizen,* September 14, 1876.

26. Robert J. Fleming to LCM, August 7, 1965. Mr. Fleming, currently president of the Colorado County Historical Society, quoting from an interview with Tommy Carrol at Alleyton, Texas, on or about August 15, 1965.

27. R. J. Fleming, quoting from an interview with Mrs. H. D. Parker.

28. C. L. Sonnichsen, *I'll Die Before I'll Run,* Devin-Adair (New York, 1962), 7.

29. Fleming, *op. cit.*

30. El Paso *Herald,* April 19, 1882.

31. Fleming, interview with John Hunter.

32. Fleming, interview with Mrs. H. D. Parker.

33. Sonnichsen, *I'll Die* 308-315.

34. Nod Clapp.

35. El Paso *Herald,* April 19, 1882.

36. United States Census, 1880, Bexar County.

37. Elizabeth Thayer (personal secretary to the late son of John Herff) to LCM, June 3, 1965.

38. El Paso *Herald,* September 27, 1882.

39. *Ibid.,* April 19, 1882.

40. John Middagh, *Frontier Newspaper, The El Paso Times,* Texas Western Press (El Paso, 1958), 1882.

41. William Coldwell, Gillett Book Review.

42. City Council Minutes, Book B, 96.

43. Frank Beaumont, El Paso *Herald,* November 27, 1909.

CHAPTER 4

1. Baylor to King, September 30, 1881, University Archives.

2. The type and position of Dallas Stoudenmire's weapons will be discussed in full during a later chapter.

3. Baylor to King, September 30, 1881, University Archives.

4. Lawrence Stevens, interview with LCM, May 25, 1966. Also, see C. L. Sonnichsen, *Pass of the North,* El Paso, TWC Press, 1968.

5. George W. Baylor, El Paso *Herald,* January 10, 1906.

6. James Gillett, *Six Years with the Texas Rangers,* 198.

7. Baylor to King, September 30, 1881, University Archives.

8. Mrs. Ester Maldonado, granddaughter of John Hale, to LCM, March 4, 1966; El Paso Census, 1880.

9. Leon Claire Metz, *John Selman: Texas Gunfighter,* Hastings House (New York 1966). 96-111.

chives.
10. Baylor to King, September 30, 1881, University Ar-

11. *Ibid.*

12. *Ibid.*

13. This is a rather slippery term to be in such common use in Mexico. It means "boss," "chief," etc. In this particular case it may even have meant "mayor" of Paso del Norte.

chives.
14. Baylor to King, September 30, 1881, University Ar-

15. Baylor was well known as a story teller and tended to write long, rambling letters about his exploits as an Indian fighter and outlaw hunter. He never hesitated to give others credit. His stories, as far as his recollection of events goes, seem to be truthful and authentic.

chives.
16. Baylor to King, September 30, 1881, University Ar-

17. George Look manuscript.

18. Alfred Schuster, interview with LCM, February 10, 1966.

19. Although Stoudenmire is generally credited with killing the innocent Mexican, a few bystanders thought that someone else may have fired the shot. Baylor, in particular, thought that Krempkau may have killed him with a wild shot. No mention officially was ever made of the incident. See George W. Baylor, El Paso *Herald,* January 10, 1906; and Zach White Diary.

chives.
20. Baylor to King, September 30, 1881, University Ar-

21. George Look manuscript.

22. *Ibid.*

23. Zach White, El Paso *Evening Post,* May 30, 1928.

24. George Look also thought that Krempkau killed Hale.

chives.
25. Baylor to King, September 30, 1881, University Ar-

26. Baylor, "Record of Scouts," June 8, 12, 16, 1881, AGF.

27. *Newman's Semi-Weekly*, Las Cruces, New Mexico, April 20, 1881.

28. Baylor to King, September 30, 1881, University Archives.

29. *Ibid.*

30. George W. Baylor, El Paso *Herald*, June 7, 1902.

31. Gillett, *Six Years* 198.

32. El Paso *Herald*, November 22, 1881. This issue of the *Herald* is quoting from an earlier edition (April 20-27), copies of which seem no longer to be in existence.

33. Reyes Medina, grandson of John Hale, interview with LCM, Canutillo, Texas, February 16, 1966.

CHAPTER 5

1. Mrs. Lois Manning (widow of Dr. George Felix Manning, Jr.), interview with LCM, Tucson, Arizona, March 24, 1966.

2. City Council Minutes, Book B, August 13, 1881.

3. Baylor to King, September 30, 1881, University Archives.

4. *Ibid.*

5. Zach White, El Paso *Evening Post*, May 30, 1928.

6. Newman's *Semi-Weekly*, April 20, 1881.

7. "Johnson was buried in a small cemetery at the corner of what later became Oregon and Missouri Streets. After a few years had passed, it became necessary to move the cemetery, and everyone gathered to see how well Old Bill had been preserved. The lid was pried off and there he lay, looking better (except for some discoloration) than some who were staring at him. Then the body collasped and turned to dust before their eyes." W. W. Bridgers, El Paso *World News*, March 7, 1924.

8. George Look MS.

9. Testimony of John Woods at inquest into the six-gun slaying of Doc Cummings. Original document in possession of author.

10. Solomon Schutz, El Paso *Herald*, January 2, 1915.

11. Newman's *Semi-Weekly*, April 20, 1881.

12. George Look MS.

13. George Look MS.

CHAPTER 6

1. Judge Allen Blacker, El Paso *Herald*, May 11, 1905.

2. Joseph Leach, "Farewell to Horse-Back, Mule-Back, Foot-Back, and Prairie Schooner: The Railroad Comes to Town," *Password* (May, 1965), 1, 34-35. Mr. Leach's article and the El Paso *Herald* for June 1, 1881, are the two best references for the railroad's entrance into El Paso.

3. James B. Gillett said Dallas Stoudenmire "had the smallest feet and hands of any person I ever saw for his size." James B. Gillett, "The Killing of Dallas Stoudenmire," *Frontier Times* (July, 1924), 1.

4. El Paso *Herald*, June 1, 1881.

5. *Ibid.*

6. The Texas Ranger muster-roll files show quite definitely that Dallas Stoudenmire was auburn headed and had hazel eyes—and was not a blonde with blue eyes as has so often been reported.

7. El Paso *Herald*, June 1, 1881.

CHAPTER 7

1. *Lone Star*, June 20, 1883.

2. *Ibid.*, March 22, 1882.

3. El Paso *Herald*, March 15, 1882.

4. Gordon Frost, interview with LCM, El Paso, September 1, 1966.

5. There is no positive evidence that Dallas Stoudenmire was left-handed; however, the fact that one photograph shows him holding a cigar in his left hand certainly indicates that this was the case. Also, Gordon Frost says that the existing Stoudenmire pistol indicates wear on the gun barrel that could only come about through being sheathed by a left-handed person.

6. "Mysterious" Dave Mather was positively identified as being in El Paso during May, 1882. He could very well have been here sooner. Baylor mentions him in his correspondence and reports, Gillett even telegraphed the governor and asked if any reward lay on Mather's head. The query was never acknowledged.

Mather did manage to remain in trouble at El Paso. He, Curly Yates, and Tom L. Davis swindled Charles Mitchell out of $50 while playing three card monte. Mitchell swore he was robbed. However, Billy Thompson (brother to Ben Thompson) convinced Mitchell (probably by threats) that he should change the robbery story to one of losing at cards. Baylor made the arrests, but Mather, Yates, and Davis were set free by a justice of the peace.

While there is no positive evidence that "Mysterious Dave" was an El Paso city marshal, this was a type of role he liked to play. Another indication of this assistant marshalship is that Stoudenmire got "very huffy" after Gillett and Baylor began looking into the fact that a reward might be out for Mather. Captain George Baylor to Captain Neal Coldwell, May 19, 1882, AGF. Also, for a thorough rundown on Mysterious Dave Mather's unsavory career, see Colin W. Rickards, "Mysterious Dave Mather," *The English Westerners Brand Book* (July, 1959), 8-12; Colin Rickards, *Mysterious Dave Mather*, The Press of the Territorian (Santa Fe, 1968).

7. City Council Minutes, Book B, 270 and 272.

8. *Lone Star*, March 25, 1882.

9. Case No. 407, 34th District Court, El Paso.

10. *Ibid.*

11. City Council Minutes, Book C., 45.

12. *Lone Star*, November 19, 1881. The El Paso *Herald* of November 22, 1881, published nearly the same story, except it said Bright was delivered to the authorities in Silver City, New Mexico.

13. *Lone Star*, October 22, 1881.

14. City Council Minutes, Book B, 166.

15. A. M. Gibson, *The Life and Death of Colonel Albert Jennings Fountain*, University of Oklahoma Press (Norman, 1965), 145-147.

16. *Lone Star*, December 14-21, 1881.

17. *Ibid.*, December 28, 1881.

18. Bartholomew to LCM, August 31, 1965.

19. The story of the Hoodoo Brown gang is told in some detail in Ed Bartholomew's, *Wyatt Earp: The Man and the Myth* (Volume 2), Frontier Book Company (Toyahvale, Texas, 1964).

20. *Lone Star*, December 31, 1881.

21. *Ibid.*, November 5, 1881.

22. *Ibid.*, December 17, 1881, and January 11, 1882.

CHAPTER 8

1. Marcus J. Wright, *Texas in the War, 1861-1865*, Hill Junior College Press (Hillsboro, Texas, 1965), 84-95; Kenneth Goldblatt, manuscript in progress on life of George W. Baylor.

2. Marshal Hail, *Knight In the Sun*, Little, Brown (Boston, 1962), 22.

3. Baylor to King, September 30, 1881, University Archives.

4. *Ibid.*

5. *Ibid.*

6. Frank Beaumont, El Paso *Herald*, November 20, 1909.

7. John B. Jones to Dallas Stoudenmire, June 1, 1881, AGF.

8. Gillett, *Six Years*, 143; Hail, *Knight In the Sun*, 20-22.

9. Nevill to Jones, February 8, 1881, University Archives.

10. Baylor to King, September 30, 1881, University Archives.

11. J. M. Deaver to J. J. Deaver, October 4, 1939.

12. Baylor to King, April 26, 1882, University Archives.

13. George Look MS. George Look, who claimed to be an eye witness (and probably was) to the Krempkau, Campbell, and Hale killings, implied that the rangers ran when the shooting started. George said that Dallas Stoudenmire and Doc Cummings (who had grabbed his shotgun and rushed out of the Globe as soon as he heard the shooting) stood in the street among the bodies and called, "Where are you rangers? Close in rangers!"

14. Baylor to King, April 26, 1882, University Archives.

15. J. M. Deaver to J. J. Deaver, October 4, 1939.

16. Frank Beaumont, El Paso *Herald*, November 20, 1909.

CHAPTER 9

1. Marriage License Records, Volume E, 400, Colorado County, Texas.

2. Mrs. Rena Savage, District Clerk of Wheeler County, to LCM, January 4, 1966. Mrs. Savage sent notarized copies of Wheeler County court records and excerpts from a book entitled *Memory Cups of Panhandle Pioneers,* by Millie Jones Porter.

3. Mrs. Rena Savage to LCM, January 4, 1966.

4. Testimony of James H. White during the pre-trial hearing of James Manning for death of S. M. Cummings.

5. El Paso *Times*, April 2, 1881.

6. *Ibid*.

7. *Ibid*.

8. Texas Ranger muster roll, G. W. Baylor, Company A, June 1 to August 31, 1881, AGF.

9. City Council minutes make several references to S. M. Cummings' being paid small sums for feeding prisoners.

10. City Council Minutes, August 2, 1881.

11. El Paso *Herald*, February 15, 1882.

12. Marriage License records, Volume F, 246, Colorado County, Texas.

13. During the inquest into Doc's death, Marshal Gillett testified that Cummings did not have any police powers. See inquest document.

14. *Ibid*., testimony of John B. Woods.

15. *Ibid*., testimony of George W. Thomas.

16. This shotgun business could be a reference to the Bill

Johnson assassination attempt on Dallas Stoudenmire, but the way it is told indicates that it refers to another incident. Incidentally, the Johnson shotgun was placed in a drug store for several days after the attempt on Stoudenmire's life. Someone stole it and it was never accounted for again.

17. Testimony of East at the inquest.

18. Testimony of Dr. J. A. McKinney at inquest.

19. *Lone Star*, February 18, 1882.

CHAPTER 10

1. Mrs. Lois Manning, widow of Dr. George Felix Manning, Jr., interview with LCM, Tucson, Arizona, March 24, 1966.

2. George W. Baylor, El Paso *Herald*, January 10, 1906.

3. Mrs. Lois Manning interview.

4. *Ibid.*

5. C. L. Sonnichsen and Mrs. William J. Coonly, interview with Frank Manning (nephew of the Manning brothers), El Paso, Texas, November 5, 1965.

6. Mrs. Lois Manning.

7. *Ibid.*

8. Robert A. Enlow, American Medical Association, to LCM, December 22, 1965.

9. Paul R. Boykin, Executive Secretary, Arizona Board of Medical Directors, to LCM, December 2, 1965.

10. Mrs. Bebe Coonly to LCM, June 24, 1965. Quoting the *Daily Arizona Miner*, January 28, 1875.

11. Bell County Marriage License Records, Volume F, 412.

12. Mrs. Lois Manning.

13. El Paso *Times*, June 1, 1881.

14. W. M. Coldwell, review of James Gillett's book.

15. City Council Minutes, Book C, 35.

16. James B. Gillett to Adjutant General King, May 20, 1882, AGF.

17. Advertisement appearing in *Lone Star*, October 19, 1881.

18. Middagh, *Frontier Newspaper*, 6.

19. City Council Minutes, Book B. August 13, 1881.

20. Baylor, Record of Scouts, October 31, 1881, AGF.

21. El Paso *Times*, April 2, 1881.

22. *Ibid.*

23. *Lone Star*, February 25, 1882.

24. Deed Record Book V, 31 and 102, El Paso County.

25. El Paso *Times*, April 2, 1881.

26. McDaniel liked to regard himself as the "Barnum of the West." Although few people took him seriously (he was considered a little eccentric due to having fallen out of a third-tier line of boxes during an altercation with a drunk), he did establish several legitimate theatres throughout the West. On account of his wife's illness, McDaniel sold out to Jim Manning and went East. He returned to El Paso to die in April, 1902. See Donald V. Brady, *The Theater In Early El Paso, 1881-1905*, TWC Southwestern Studies, Monograph No. 13, Volume IV, No. 1, 1966.

27. El Paso *Times*, January 1, 1882.

28. *Lone Star*, December 14, 1881.

29. J. M. Deaver to J. J. Deaver, October 4, 1939.

30. Reprinted in the El Paso *Herald* on September 20, 1882.

CHAPTER 11

1. El Paso *Times*, January 1, 1882.

2. James B. Gillett, El Paso *Herald*, August 14, 1909.

3. Never one to resist an impulse to pat himself on the back, Mills wrote that in the annals of great literature, he felt that *Forty Years In El Paso* ranked tenth. He modestly admitted that the Bible, Shakespeare, Mark

Twain, and a few others did edge him out. This information taken from random papers in the W. W. Mills collection, University Archives.

4. City Council Minutes, Book B, 182.

5. W. W. Bridgers, "A Frontier Missionary Was Parson Tays," El Paso *Times*, June 17, 1940.

6. It was common practice for the marshal to attend all council meetings.

7. City Council Minutes, Book C, 4-5.

8. *Ibid.*, page 46; *Lone Star*, March 29, 1882.

9. City Council Minutes, Book C, 61; *Lone Star*, April 5, 1882.

10. City Council Minutes, Book C, 61-63; *Lone Star*, April 8, 1882.

11. W. W. Mills, *Forty Years In El Paso*, Revised Edition, published by Carl Hertzog (El Paso, 1962), 159-164.

12. *Lone Star*, April 8, 1882.

13. Middagh, *Frontier Newspaper*, 8-9.

14. Oddly enough, the council minutes make no mention of the Stoudenmire trouble during this meeting—nor do they even mention that Stoudenmire's resignation is desired. For the full story it was necessary to go to the newspapers.

15. Judge Blacker speaking before a meeting of the El Paso Pioneer Society. El Paso *Herald*, May 11, 1905.

16. City Council Minutes, Book C, 72.

17. *Lone Star*, May 31, 1882.

18. Baylor to King, May 31, 1882, University Archives.

CHAPTER 12

1. El Paso *Herald* May 13, 1882. An advertisement in this newspaper read that Dallas Stoudenmire was selling the Globe to Narrie R. Pierce. On December 20, the *Lone Star* reported a gentlemen from Ysleta had purchased the Globe and planned to convert it to a grocery store.

2. Emolument account for Hal L. Gosling for half of year ending December 31, 1882, National Archives and Records Service.

3. William Page, like many violent men of this era, came to an unhappy end. The *Lone Star* of May 30, 1883, recorded the story of Page's final days as a prospector near San Augustin in the Organ Mountains of New Mexico.

"Page and Matlock were playing cards in [Kinney and Carr's] saloon and drinking heavily. A dispute arose over the game and Page jumped up, slapped Matlock, and then went to the bar to get his revolver and shoot him. Carr said he would get no pistol and retreated to the end of the bar followed by Page, who stooped to pick up a large knife under the counter. Seeing this, Carr pulled a revolver and as Page advanced toward him, knife in hand, shot him twice, killing him instantly. Carr was examined the next day by a justice of the peace and acquitted."

4. Gillett, *Six Years*, 237; El Paso *Times*, July 29, 1882.

5. El Paso *Herald*, April 9, 1895.

6. *Ibid.*

7. Some accounts say he had been in Lordsburg and Silver City, New Mexico—others say Tucson, Arizona.

8. C. C. Brooks is the authority for this conversation. Testimony before Justice of the Peace E. S. Johnson, September 19, 1882.

9. *Ibid.*

CHAPTER 13

1. Testimony of A. L. Nichols as printed in the Colorado County *Citizen*, September 28, 1882. The *Citizen* quoted from the El Paso *Times*, but this particular issue of the *Times* has been lost or destroyed.

2. *Lone Star*, September 20, 1882. Mayor Magoffin and Judge Blacker were preparing warrants for both Stoudenmire and the Manning brothers.

3. Testimony of C. C. Brooks, El Paso *Herald*, September 20, 1882; testimony of J. W. Jones, Colorado County *Citizen*, September 28, 1882. The original court records containing this testimony are missing from the files and reliance has to be placed on the newspaper versions.

4. S. H. Newman, editor of the *Lone Star*, scribbled a description of the gun in the back of a copy of Mills' *Forty Years in El Paso*.

CHAPTER 14

1. One Mexican bystander was nicked in the hand by a stray ball. *Lone Star*, September 23, 1882.

2. One of the blows tore a wound an inch long in Stoudenmire's scalp. El Paso *Herald*, September 20, 1882.

3. Verdict as written by the El Paso *Herald*, September 20, 1882; and by Colorado County *Citizen*, September 28, 1882.

4. Case nos. 443 and 444, 34th District Court.

5. Case nos. 502 and 512, 34th District Court.

6. *Lone Star*, February 25, 1885.

7. Mrs. Lois Manning.

8. El Paso *Herald*, July 26, 1882; November 8, 1882.

9. *Lone Star*, May 26, 1883; June 2, 1883.

10. *Ibid.*, May 26, 1883.

11. Mrs. Lois Manning.

12. Medical Records Dept., Arizona State Hospital to LCM, May 24, 1966.

13. Mrs. Gladys Lombardo, Interview with LCM, El Paso, 1968.

14. Enlow to LCM, December 22, 1965.

15. This is believed to be the same Charlie Utter who was such a close friend of James Butler "Wild Bill" Hickok. Utter, known primarily for the fact that he took a bath every day (a rarity in the West), spent a little time in Texas and was closely associated with Eleanor Dumont, *alias* Minnie the Gambler, who died in El Paso in 1904. Also, Charlie's brother Steve supposedly served several years as a Texas Ranger.

16. *Lone Star*, March 24-28, 1883.

17. Baylor to Captain Jno. O. Johnson, August 6, 1883, AGF.

18. Joe Evans, interview with LCM, June 10, 1966.

19. For another look at Gillett's life, see Mildred Cox Shannon, *James B. Gillett, Indomitable Texan*, a thesis for a Masters Degree presented to Sul Ross State College (Alpine, Texas), August, 1960.

CHAPTER 15

1. John W. Denny, *A Century of Freemasonry at El Paso*, Texas Western Press (El Paso, 1965), 48.

2. Virginia was under the impression that her brother Dallas was due several hundred dollars from the United States government. Stoudenmire's Emolument account, however, states that he earned only $275 of which $175 had been paid. See Marshal Hal Gosling, Emolument account ending 1882, National Archives.

3. Probate Case No. 41, September 30 and October 3, 1882.

4. Mrs. Abbabell Everett, interview with LCM, July 1, 1965; letter to LCM, July 13, 1965.

5. Colorado County *Citizen*, September 28, 1882.

6. Virginia Stoudenmire and her children (number and sex unknown) dropped out of sight, and all efforts to trace them have been unsuccessful.

At Columbus on December 5, 1883, Belle Stoudenmire married Charles S. Kerl. Kerl, supposedly a railroader, spent considerable time in Mexico. He and Belle had several children, all of whom seem to have vanished from history.

7. *Lone Star*, August 5-9, 1882.

BIBLIOGRAPHY

Books and Articles

Bartholomew, Ed.   *Wyatt Earp: The Man and the Myth.* Fort Davis, Texas: Frontier Book Company, 1964.

Black, James M.   *The Families and Descendants in America of Golsan, Golson, Gholson, and Gholston.* Salt Lake City: James M. Black, 1959.

Brady, Donald V.   *The Theatre In Early E. Paso, 1881-1905.* Southwest Studies, Monograph No. 13. Texas Western Press: El Paso, Texas, 1966.

Calleros, Cleofas   *El Paso Missions and Indians.* El Paso, Texas: McMath Company, 1951.

Denny, John W.   *A Century of Freemasonry at El Paso.* El Paso, Texas; Texas Western Press, 1965.

Gibson, A. M.   *The Life and Death of Colonel Albert Jennings Fountain.* Norman: University of Oklahoma Press, 1965.

Gillett, James B.   *Six Years With the Texas Rangers,* Yale University Press, 1925.

"The Killing of Dallas Stoudenmire." *Frontier Times*, (July, 1924).

Hail, Marshal   *Knight in the Sun*. Boston: Little, Brown and Company, 1962.

Kemp, Ben W.   *Cow Dust and Saddle Leather*. Norman: University of
and J. C. Dykes   Oklahoma Press, 1968.

Leach, Joseph   "Farewell to Horseback, Muleback, Footback, and Prairie Schooner: The Railroad Comes to Town." *Password*, El Paso Historical Society Publication, El Paso, Texas, May 1965.

Metz, Leon Claire ✓ *John Selman: Texas Gunfighter*. New York, Hastings House, 1966.

Middagh, John   *Frontier Newspaper: The El Paso Times*. El Paso, Texas: Texas Western Press, 1958.

Mills, W. W.   *Forty Years in El Paso*. El Paso, Texas: Revised Edition, Carl Hertzog, 1962.

Rickards, Colin W.   "Mysterious Dave Mather." *The English Westerners Brand Books*; July, 1959.

                      Mysterious Dave Mather. Santa Fe: the Press of the Territorian, 1968.

Sonnichsen, C. L.   *Ten Texas Feuds*. Albuquerque: University of New Mexico Press, 1957.

                      Pass of the North, El Paso, Texas, TWC Press, 1968.

                      El Paso Salt War. El Paso, Texas: Carl Hertzog and the Texas Western Press, 1961.

                      I'll Die Before I'll Run. New York: Devin-Adair, 1962.

Wise, Clyde, Jr.   "The Effects of the Railroad Upon El Paso." *Password* May 1965.

Wright, Marcus J.   *Texas In the War, 1861-1865*. Hillsboro, Texas: Hill Junior College Press, 1965.

Manuscript Material

Deaver, J. M.   An old Texas Ranger writes his kinsman on October 4, 1939, giving his version of Stoudenmire's difficulties and death. Copy in possession of author.

Goldblatt, Kenneth *George Baylor, Ranger Captain*, MS.

Look, George   Typescript account of some early El Paso gunfights, written by an eye witness. Original in the files of the late Maury Kemp. Copy in possession of author, courtesy Wyndham White.

Richardson, Charles. Letter addressed to the U. S. State Department, October 14, 1881, in file entitled "Dispatches From Unites States Consuls in Ciudad Juarez." Microfilm copy in possession of Library at The University of Texas at El Paso.

Shannon, Mildred Cox. *James B. Gillett, Indomitable Texan*, M.A. thesis, Sul Ross State College (Alpine, Texas), August, 1960.

Sonnichsen, C. L.   *Pass of the North*, El Paso: Texas Western Press.

White, Zach   Personal diary in possession of Mr. White's daughter, Mrs. Paul Harvey.

                    Adjutant General's File, Texas State Library, Austin. Nearly all of the official Texas Ranger files are preserved here.

                    El Paso City Council Minutes, typescript, the El Paso Public Library.

                    Habeas Corpus proceedings in the slaying of Samuel M. "Doc" Cummings by James Manning. The file contains sixty-three pages of hand-written affidavits in regard to the shooting and several very crude drawings of the interior of the bar section of the Coliseum Variety Theater. Original document in possession of author.

                    National Archives and Records Service, Washington, D.C., holds most of the Civil War records of participants in the Stoudenmire story.

                    University Archives, The University of Texas at Austin. The late Walter Prescott Webb collected most of the Texas Ranger reports, sorted them, and converted them into typescripts.

Miscellaneous Documentary Material

                    Federal Census, Macon County, Alabama, 1850.

                    Federal Census, Pike County, Alabama, 1860.

Federal Census, El Paso County, Texas, 1880.

Marriage License Records, Volume E, 400, Colorado County, Texas. Marriage of Stanley M. "Doc" Cummings to Virginia May (Stoudenmire).

Marriage License Records, Volume F, 412, Bell County, Texas. Marriage of George Felix "Doc" Manning to Sarah E. Alexander.

Marriage License Records, Volume F, 246, Colorado County, Texas. Marriage of Dallas Stoudenmire to Isabella Sherrington.

Deed Record Book, Volume V, 31 & 102. Frank Manning leases his saloon from Mrs. Juana Dowell.

Case No. 407, 34th District Court, El Paso, Texas. Trial of William Page for assault upon "Arab."

Case Nos. 443 and 444, 34th District Court, El Paso, Texas. Court trials of George Felix and James Manning for murder of Dallas Stoudenmire.

Case Nos. 502 and 512, 34th District Court, El Paso, Texas. James Manning charged with swindling and misapplication of county funds.

Probate Case No. 41, September 30 and October 3, 1882, El Paso County, Texas. Virginia Cummings, Dallas Stoudenmire's sister, is given custody of Stoudenmire's property and debts.

Probate Case No. 41, September 30 and October 3, 1882, El Paso County, Texas Virginia Cummings, Dallas Stoudenmire's sister, is given charge of Stoudenmire's property and debts.

Newspaper

Colorado County Citizen

Daily Arizona Miner

El Paso *Evening Post*

El Paso *Herald*

El Paso *Times*

El Paso *World News*

Las Vegas (New Mexico) *Optic*

El Paso *Lone Star*

Newman's *Semi-Weekly* (Las Cruces, New Mexico)

ACKNOWLEDGMENTS

S O MUCH credit is due those who contributed in some fashion to this book, that if the entire list were printed, along with their contributions, more space would be required than is given over to the actual story.

Nevertheless, my gratitude goes out to C. L. Sonnichsen, a generous and understanding friend who taught me both the joys and techniques of historical research.

Another close friend, Francis Fugate, donated hours in giving me the frank benefit of his vast critical and literary knowledge.

To the UTEP and the El Paso Public Library I shall be forever indebted. In particular, I wish to thank Baxter Polk, the Librarian at UTEP and his two fine assistants, Frank Scott, head UTEP and James Cleveland. Words can never express my appreciation to Mrs. Virginia Hoke, head of the Southwest Room, and Mrs. Emma Hamilton, Southwest Reference clerk at the El Paso Public Library.

No friend could have been of more assistance than Commander Millard McKinney, USN, Ret. Together we chewed over many a Stoudenmire point of view.

Mrs. Bebe Coonly, renouned Southwest artist, was always ready with time and information concerning the Southwest.

Kenneth Goldblatt, a superb researcher, turned up material in the Adjutant General's File in Austin that I never dreamed existed. Ken was kind enough to share it with me.

My old "compadre," Gordon Frost, allowed me to browse through his home and view the finest collection of firearms in America. To Gordon, a special note of appreciation.

My corresponding friend and fellow writer and historian Ed Bartholomew was more than generous as he combed out and sent me many excerpts from his massive Southwest files.

Probably one of the finest, yet least known, Mexican and Southwest collectors is R. T. "Dick" Copenbarger of El Paso. Dick, a long-time personal friend, found and gave to me the inquest proceedings dealing with the death of Doc Cummings.

Robert J. Fleming, President of the Colorado County Historical Society, worked hard in cold-trailing Stoudenmire's career in East Texas. He did an excellent job.

Frank Manning, El Paso County Sheriff's office, gave me hours of his time in discussing the Manning brothers.

The staff of the El Paso District Clerk's office and the El Paso County Clerk's offices came through with much assistance in ferretting out local records pertaining to Dallas Stoudenmire. In particular, I wish to thank Bill Johnson, Earl Forsyth, and Wally Fields.

Others who contributed in a large measure to this book are Carey Haigler, Charlotte, North Carolina; Mrs. Alex Stoudenmire, Prattville, Alabama; James Black, Salt Lake City, Utah; Mrs. Florence Alley Parker, Alleyton, Texas; Nod Clapp, El Campo, Texas; Mrs. Rena Savage, Wheeler County, Texas; Chester V. Kielman, Austin; James Day, Austin; R. N. "Bob" Mullin, South Laguna, California; Bob McCubbin, El Paso, Bud Newman, Dr. Rex Strickland, Carl Hertzog, Chris Fox, and Joe Evans, all of El Paso.

A special note of thanks to Adamarie Pastrana and her mother Gladys Lombardo for the Manning photos, plus additional and long sought information on the brothers.

INTERVIEWS AND PERSONAL CORRESPONDENCE

In my files are well over one hundred letters, most of which are unmentioned in the footnotes. Yet they all proved invaluable, and without them the true saga of Dallas Stoudenmire would be incomplete. To these unacknowledged contributors, my sincere appreciation and gratitude.

D. D. Cusenbary (Young County, Texas, Treasurer) to LCM, August 12, 1966; Mrs. Alex Stoudenmire to LCM, July 4, July 28, 1966; Carey E. Haigler to LCM, July 3, November 11, September 12, 1965 (Mr. Haigler is a descendant of the Stoudenmires); James M. Black to LCM, February 10, 1966 (Mr. Black is also a relative of the Stoudenmires); Peter Brannon (Director of Alabama Archives) to LCM, December 12, 1965; Walker M. Love (Senior Archivist, Tennessee State Archives) to LCM, February 2, 1966; Robert J. Fleming (President of Colorado County, Texas, Historical Society) to LCM, August 7, 1965; Nod Clapp, El Campo, Texas (his mother remembered Dallas Stoudenmire), telephone interview, November 27, 1965; Elizabeth Thayer (personal secretary to the late son of Dr. John Herff) to LCM, June 3, 1965; Lawrence Stevens, El Paso, Texas, (Mr. Stevens has a barrel of El Paso information that he easily remembers) interview with LCM, May 25, 1966; Mrs. Easter Maldonado (granddaughter of John Hale) to LCM, March 4, 1966; Alfred Schuster, El Paso (Mr. Schuster is the son of B. Schuster) interview with LCM, February 10, 1966; Reyes Medina (grandson of John Hale), El Paso, Texas, interview with LCM, February 16, 1966; Mrs. Lois Manning (widow of George Felix Manning, Jr.), Tucson, Arizona, interview with LCM March 24, 1966; Gordon Frost (personal friend who has a Stoudenmire pocket pistol in his huge firearms collection), El Paso, Texas, interview with LCM September 1, 1966; Mrs. Rena Savage (District Clerk of Wheeler County, Texas) to LCM, January 4, 1966; Robert A. Enlow (American Medical Association) to LCM, December 22, 1965; Paul Boykin (Executive Secretary of Arizona Board of Medical Directors) to LCM, December 2, 1965; Mrs. Abbabell Everett (resident of Colorado County, Texas) to LCM, June 24, 1965; Mrs. Florence Alley Parker (old-time resident of Alleyton, Texas) to LCM, February 5, 1966; and Mrs. Bebe Coonly (artist and Southwest researcher) El Paso, Texas, letter to LCM, June 24, 1965.

INDEX

−A−

Abbie Bell's parlor house: 112
Aberfoil, Ababama: 24
Abeytia: 72
Acme Saloon: 85, 102, 110, 112, 114, 116
Alabama: 93
Alabama Cavalry: 26
Alabama University: 93
Alamo Saloon: 81
Alarcon, Jose: 68
Albuquerque: 110
Alexander, Sarah E.: 95
Allen, Frank: 20, 23
Alleyton, Texas: 28, 29, 30, 126
Anacortes, Washington: 123
Apaches: 12, 57
Arab: 65
Arizona: 58, 122
Arizona Brigade: 70
Arizona State Hospital: 123
Arzate, Leonor Isabelle: 124
Atchison, Topeka, and Santa Fe Railroad: 59
Austin, Texas: 121

−B−

Bartholomew, Ed: 68
Bassett, Private: 76
Baylor, George W.: 3, 5, 6-9, 36-39, 44-49, 54, 70-79, 85
Bean, Col.: 57
Beaumont, Frank: 9, 33, 49, 52, 73, 80, 81
Beebe, Pearl: 18
Bell, Billy: 110
Belle: 98
"bellygun": 62
Belton, Texas: 94
Bernardo Prairie: 29
Big Dal: 68
Big Tony: 68
Blacker, Alderman: 107
Blacker, Judge: 57, 58, 107
Blum, Ike: 97, 120
Bond, Private: 76
Bragg, General: 26
Bright, Joe E.: 65
Brooks, C. C.: 111, 114, 115
Brooks, bartender: 116
Brothers, Mr.: 15

Brown County: 27
Brown, Jane: 17
Brown, W. E.: 57
Buckler, Judge: 40, 41
Burns, Hannah: 15

−C−

Cain, J. C.: 20, 22, 39
Calle Comercio: 12
Calle 16th de Septiembre: 12
Caldwell, Neal: 73
California: 58
Campbell: 92, 96-98
Campbell, George: 3, 4, 6-8, 38,
    40-43, 49, 50, 76, 96, 126
Campbell, R. F.: 99
Canada: 58
Canutillo Gang: 37
Canutillo Road: 45
Carleton's California Column: 38
Carrie: 112, 114
Carrico, George Washington: 84, 105
Central Hotel: 59, 84, 104
Chicago: 85
Chihuahua, Mexico: 86
Chinese coolies: 55, 56
Chipman, Ranger Herman: 72, 76
Chisum, John: 38
Citizen, Juan Q.: 58
"City Marshal, El Paso, Texas": 124
Civil War: 71, 93
Clark, Etta: 17, 18
Clapp, Mrs.: 31
Cobweb Saloon: 112
Coldwell, W. M.: 3, 4, 86
Coleman, Jim: 30
Coliseum Saloon: 17, 88, 97
Coliseum Variety Theater: 87
Colorado County: 27-29, 86, 125
Colorado County *Citizen*: 31
Columbus, Texas: 82, 86, 125
Comanches: 12
Commerce Street: 12
Comstock, Assistant Marshal: 15, 119
Concordia Cemetery: 14, 47, 110
Confederate Army: 25, 26
Corre, John: 83
Copeland, Ed: 8, 9
Corpus Christi, Texas: 122
Cox, Hugh: 20

Crocker, Charles F.: 57
Cummings and Company: 92
Cummings, Julia: 94
Cummings, Samuel M. "Doc": 31,
    42, 51-53, 59, 74, 82-92
Cummings, Virginia: 125

−D−

Dampin, Sgt. W. M.: 49
Danipien, Pvt.: 9
Davenport, Gipsie: 15
Davis, Les: 20, 23
Dawson, Frank: 63
Deaver, J. M.: 77, 119
De Janutt, M. B.: 63, 64
De Janutt, Nep: 80
Deming, New Mexico: 46, 53, 56, 65,
    76, 111
Deming, Texas: 57
Denny, John: 125
Denver: 85
De Ouate, Don Juan: 12
Dona Ana County: 69
Dona Ana County Sheriff: 69
Doniphan, Colonel: 13
Dougher, John: 66
Dowell, B. S.: 2
Dowell Saloon, Ben: 97
Doyle's Concert Hall: 110
Doyle's, Johnny, Saloon: 53
Doyle's Place, Johnny: 56
Duke, Benton: 30
Duke, "Little": 30

−E−

East Texas: 95
East, T. H.: 88
Edwards, Shelton: 82-84
El Paso *Herald*: 59, 60, 114
El Paso Hotel: 97
El Paso Railway: 5, 69
El Paso Salt War: 2
El Paso Street: 2, 34, 40, 41, 43, 44,
    51-53, 89, 97
El Paso *Times*: 10, 14, 18, 84, 105
El Paso Valley: 58
Erath County, Texas: 27
Evans, Jesse: 38

—F—

Fannin Hotel, Houston, Texas: 71
Felix, George: 93, 94
"Fence Cutting War": 71
Fitch, Ed: 39, 40, 49
Flood, Noah H.: 100, 106, 107
Forest Lawn Cemetery: 123
Fort Bliss: 58, 73
Fort Gibson, Indian Territory: 70
Fort Worth, Texas: 62
Forty Years in El Paso: 101
Franklin: 13
Franklin Mountains: 19, 44
Frank's Saloon: 96
Freemasons, Lodge No. 130, A.F. & F.M.: 125
Frontier Battalion: 74
Frost, Gordon: 62

—G—

Gadden, Gen. James: 55
Garrett, Pat: 110
Gem Saloon: 17, 97, 115, 120
German and Company, E.: 80
Gholson (see Golson) family: 25
Giddings, Lee County, Texas: 94
Gillett, James B.: 3, 7, 15, 37, 39, 44-46, 54, 65-68, 75-77, 86 92, 96, 103, 105, 107, 109, 119, 123, 124
Gilson: 87
Globe Restaurant: 41, 51, 52, 85, 86, 89, 109
Gonzales, Sheriff: 120
Goode: 38
Golson, Lewis: 25
Gosling, Hal L.: 109, 111, 121
Gulf Coast: 94
Guzman, Adela: 15, 16

—H—

Hague, James: 32, 58, 65, 99-101, 104
Hale, Johnny, Ranch: 7, 22, 37-40, 42-44, 46, 49, 50, 76, 92, 96, 98, 126
Hall, W. R.: 120
Hardy, Dick: 84
Harrison, Corporal: 9
Harrison, J. F.: 99

Harshaw, Arizona: 69
Hart, Antonio: 2
Hathaway, C. L.: 79
Hays County: 38
Heiff, Dr. John: 31
Hickok, W. T.: 85
Hogan, F. V.: 99
Hood: 67
Hoodoo Brown: 68
Hoover, Buck: 30
Hoover, Tuck: 30
Hot Springs: 111
Houston, East and West Texas Railroad Co.: 84
Howard, Tillie: 18
Hueco Mountains: 14
Huntsville, Alabama: 93

—I—

I'll Die Before I'll Run: 29
Indian marauding party: 95
Irvin's Drug: 51

—J—

Johnson, Bill (William): 3, 7, 9, 10, 32, 33, 50, 51, 86, 92
Johnson, Ranger William (not Bill): 8
Johnson, Justice of the Peace: 65
Johnson, J.: 62, 76
Johnson, ex-marshal: 87
Johnston, Albert Sidney's staff: 70
Johnston, Gen. Joe: 26
Jones, A. S.: 63
Jones, Major John B.: 5, 28, 54, 63, 71, 75, 116, 117, 126
Juarez: 12
Juarique: 39
Jumano Indians: 11

—K—

Kollenberg, Dr. Alex: 67
Kansas: 86, 95
Kansas Sheriff: 86
Kaplan's store: 119
Keating, Paul's Saloon: 40-42, 44, 56, 73, 124
Kentuckian: 100
King, General: 50, 74, 108
King, Joe: 20, 69
Kling, David: 89, 90

Kraukauer, A.: 2, 7
Krempkau, Gus: 41-43, 46, 76

–L–

Lake Valley Authorities: 67
Lake Valley, New Mexico: 66
Lamy, New Mexico: 68
Lamy thug: 68
Las Cruces: 45, 69
Las Vegas, New Mexico: 110
Las Vegas, New Mexico, *Optic*: 13, 14
Law and Order League: 53
Lawrence, Charlie: 42
Leadville, Colorado: 97
Leach, Fred: 110
Lloyd, Corporal: 7, 9
Lone Star: 15-18, 21, 61, 80, 98, 105
Look, George: 18-21, 44
Loring, Fred: 121, 122
Los Angeles: 123
Love, Verdie: 17
Lufkin, Dave: 67

–Mc–

McDaniel, J. A.: 97
McGonegal, Lt.: 56
McKinney, Dr. J. A.: 90
McMasters: 84

–M–

Macon County, Alabama: 24, 82
Magoffin, Joseph: 2, 8, 32, 46, 57, 64, 65, 73, 74, 101, 104, 107
Magoffinsville: 13
Manning Brothers: 20, 37, 38, 44, 48, 50, 53, 54, 76, 88, 105, 111, 114, 124
Manning and Hale: 38
"Mannings, damn": 86
Manning, Frank: 90, 93, 95-97, 99, 111, 114, 115, 122, 123
Manning, George Felix "Doc": 20, 27, 37, 93-97, 99, 115-117, 119, 120, 123
Manning, Jim: 77, 86-93, 95-99, 113, 119, 120, 123
Manning, John: 93, 95-97, 120-122

Manning, Peyton Thomas: 93
Manning, William: 93, 95
Manning's, Jim, Coliseum: 76
Manning's Saloon: 51, 52, 56, 76, 81, 88, 112, 119
Mansfield, battle of: 70
Marcuses' Jewelry: 90
Marfa, Texas: 124
Marsh Ranch: 6
Marsh's, Mrs. boarding house: 69
Marshall, Sherman: 104
Masonic Caledonia Lodge, No. 68, A.F. & F.M., of Columbus: 126
Mathis, H. M.: 64
Maximilian: 94
May, Mr. I. C. B: 82
May, Virginia Stoudenmire: 82
Medical College of Alabama: 94
Mentz, Texas: 28, 29
Mesa Avenue: 17, 102
Mesa Gardens: 126
Mesilla, New Mexico: 53, 55, 69, 84
Mexican authorities: 67
Mexico: 36, 75, 87, 94
Mills, W. W.: 101, 103, 104, 120
Mission de Nuestra Senora de Guadalupe: 13
Milton, George: 27
Moesner, Chris: 66, 67
Molett, Dr.: 94, 95
Mundy's Market: 51
Mundy's Ranch: 44
Myers, Ann: 17

–N–

Neill, G. F.: 18, 41
Neis, Deputy United States Marshal Tony: 68
Nevill, Lt. C. L.: 75
New Braunfels, Texas: 121
New Mexico (territory): 11, 36, 58, 75, 84, 104
Newman, Simeon: 16
Newman, Editor: 105
Nibsy: 20
Nichols, A. L.: 115, 116
Nolan County: 71
North Carolina: 26, 82
Northwest Texas: 75

–O–

Occidental Saloon: 8
Ochoa, T. D.: 2, 112
Ochoa, Don Ynocente: 39
O'Connell, Eugene: 18
Oldham County: 31, 82
O'Neal: 39
O'Neal, Frank: 20, 22
Optic: 68
Orcas, Island: 123
Overland Building: 43, 73, 85
Overland Street: 34

–P–

Page, William M.: 64, 65, 89, 110
Paladins: 71
Palmer, May: 18
Panhandle: 31, 74
Palace Drug Store: 96
Parda, Jesus: 71
Paris, France: 93
Parker, Arizona: 123
Paso del Norte Hotel: 97
Paso del Norte, Mexico: 12, 34, 35,
    58, 59, 85, 97
Paxton, Dr.: 69
Peterson, Lum (or Lem): 38
Peveler, Chris: 8, 38-44, 44-46, 76
Phillips, Alderman: 107
Pierce, President: 55
Piro Indians: 11
Pitts, James: 121
Pleasant Hills, Battle of: 71
Police Gazette: 84
Ponce de Leon, Juan Maria: 13
Pony Saloon: 116
Pruess, Judge: 14
Procter, Mr. and Mrs.: 69
Provencio, Don Espiridon: 58
Provencio, Eulalio: 67

–R–

Raitt, Charles: 69
Rancho Angelita: 47
Rand, Major Noyes: 32, 53
Red River Campaign of 1864: 70
Richardson, Charles C.: 20
Riley, Colorado County Judge
    Charles: 86
Rincon, New Mexico: 68, 69

Rio Bravo: 12
Rio Grande Lodge, No. 23, Knights
    of Pythias: 91
Rio Grande Railway: 5
Rio Grande River: 12, 36, 44, 58, 86
Roberts, Governor: 4
Rodgers, J. W.: 63
Ross, Dr. King: 90
Ryan, Patrick: 20, 21

–S–

Salt War: 13, 72
St. Clement's, Church of: 102
San Antonio Express: 32
San Antonio Street: 2, 3, 5, 40, 85
San Antonio, Texas: 71, 72
San Augustin, New Mexico: 45
San Elizario: 58
San Francisco Street: 3
San Marcial, New Mexico: 84
Sanchez: 39
Santa Anna: 55
Santa Fe, New Mexico: 104
Schuster, Ben: 18, 40, 41, 53, 54, 67
Schuster's Store: 53
Schutz Hall: 58
Schutz, Mayor: 7, 8, 104, 107
Schutz, Solomon: 2, 8, 53
Scott, Frank: 76, 77
Scotten, Ed: 76, 80, 119
Seattle, Washington: 123
Selman, John: 38
Seven Rivers, New Mexico: 38
Shea, Pat: 43, 44
Sherman, Marshal John: 104
Sherrington, Miss Isabella: 86
Six Years with the Texas Rangers: 3
Slade, S. C.: 2
Smith: 45
Smugglers' Pass: 37
Socorro, Ysleta: 58, 72
Sonnichsen, C. L.: 29
South America: 94
South Carolina: 25, 82
Southerland, Henry: 72
Southern Development Company: 57
Southern Pacific Railway: 5, 34,
    55-57, 96
Sparks Boys: 30
Sprinz: 64
Starr, Cleo: 18
State National Bank: 51

Stevens, A. I.: 4
Stevens County: 27
Stevenson, Frank: 38-40, 44-46
Stoudenmire, Abednego: 24, 27
Stoudenmire, Ann Alabama: 24
Stoudenmire, Belle: 125
Stoudenmire, Colonel: 27
Stoudenmire, Elizabeth Leger (or Seger): 24, 25
Stoudenmire, John M.: 24
Stoudenmire, Lewis: 24, 25
Stoudenmire, Marshal: 57, 59
Stoudenmire, Meshak: 24
Stoudenmire, Morgan: 24
Stoudenmire, Samuel: 24
Stoudenmire, Virginia M.: 24, 25, 59, 82
Stromblatt: 122

−T−

Tarde: 124
Tays, John B.: 2, 3, 72, 102
Texas Rangers: 71, 82
Thompson, Frank: 20, 21, 39, 122
Tigua Indians: 11
Times, The: 96
Tiboli Hall: 106
Tompiro Indians: 11
Tong Wars: 56
True, Mr.: 10
Truth or Consequences, New Mexico: 26
Turbo, Kirk: 77
Tucker, Dan: 46
Tucson Division: 57

−U−

United States: 58
United States Government: 125
Upshur County, Texas: 27
Utah Street: 17
Utter, Charlie: 124

−V−

Vanston (bartender): 44
Variety Theatre: 17, 76, 97

−W−

Wade, Mr.: 89
Waldie, Ranger Joe: 73
Wallace, Big Foot: 32
Wallace, Will: 38
Waller, Capt. J. R.: 27, 28
Walz, Mr.: 122
Washington Park: 56
Weldon, T. L.: 8, 38-40, 76
Wharton, John Austin: 71
Wheeler County: 31, 74, 82
Wheeler, General Joe: 93
White, James H.: 69, 84, 121, 122, 127
White, Zach: 44
Wilson, Private: 9
Wombold: 69
Woods, John: 2, 3, 86

−Y−

Yeager, Charles: 121
Ysleta: 3, 35, 37, 76, 79, 85
Ysleta Rangers Camp: 72